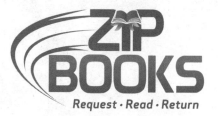

Between Harlem AND Heaven

AFRO-ASIAN-AMERICAN COOKING FOR
BIG NIGHTS, WEEKNIGHTS, & EVERY DAY

ALSO BY ALEXANDER SMALLS

Grace the Table: Stories and Recipes from My Southern Revival

AFRO-ASIAN-AMERICAN COOKING FOR
BIG NIGHTS, WEEKNIGHTS, & EVERY DAY

Between Harlem AND Heaven

JJ JOHNSON AND ALEXANDER SMALLS

with Veronica Chambers

PHOTOGRAPHY BY
Beatriz da Costa

FLATIRON
BOOKS

FOOD STYLING BY
Roscoe Betsill

NEW YORK

DEDICATED TO THE

BRILLIANT CULINARY LEGACY

OF THE AFRICAN PEOPLE

THROUGHOUT THE DIASPORA

· ·

· ·

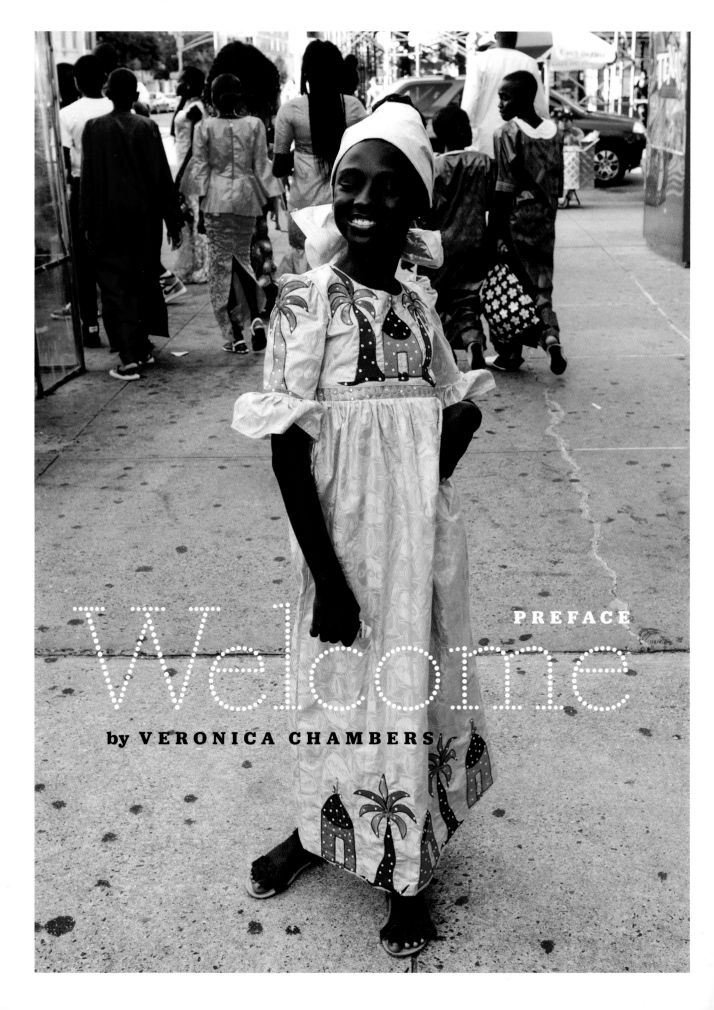

Welcome

PREFACE

by VERONICA CHAMBERS

Harlem makes you hungry. For food. For art. For music. For street style. For history. For old people. For young people. For kids playing basketball that's so good that pro players hit the courts during their off hours. For girls who jump rope with so many flips and so much gymnastic flair that every other sidewalk feels like an Olympic arena.

Directions on how to get to Harlem inspired one of the most famous jazz standards of our time. In 1939, Duke Ellington offered a young musician named Billy Strayhorn a place in his orchestra. He sent him money to travel, by train, from Pittsburgh to New York City. Once Strayhorn arrived in New York City, Ellington instructed him how to get to his home in Harlem: Take the A train. Strayhorn turned the directions into a song and it became a beloved tune that was the signature of Duke Ellington's orchestra.

Ella Fitzgerald recorded the song more than a dozen times, and you can her live version, complete with her signature scatting, on *Ella in Hollywood.* The song has been recorded and performed by artists as diverse as Charles Mingus, Chaka Khan, Phish, and the Rolling Stones.

It's as true now as it was back in 1939: To get to Duke Ellington's Harlem, you take the A train. (You can also take the B or the C.) When you get there, you'll want to head directly to Minton's, but don't rush and don't, if you can help it, Uber there. You don't want door-to-door service when you're coming to Harlem to eat. You want to take it all in. Let Harlem make you hungry first.

Harlem is where we met and began to create the culinary journey that is this book. You have to understand that Alexander's home is one of Harlem's most revered salons. Drop by any given Sunday and you will find movie stars and musicians, architects and athletes. Alexander spent decades traveling the globe as a Tony Award–winning opera singer, and offstage, he began to mix the low-country cooking of his South Carolina roots with dishes and flavors from all across the African diaspora. JJ was an up-and-coming chef who had been trained in classic European techniques but longed to bring to the table the influences of his Caribbean childhood and all the ways that brought Asia and Africa together on the plate. Using Alexander's kitchen as a laboratory, the two men began to create the Afro-Asian-American flavor profile that comprises this book. Instead of the traditional mother sauces of France, they whipped up a peanut sauce they called the Mother Africa sauce. They served citrus jerk bass with a West African grain called fonio. They served spiced goat onigiri style, enshrined in a square of sticky rice. Oxtail dumplings in a green apple curry was something they'd never seen on any other menu, but it was beautiful to the eye and even more delicious to taste

Together, Alexander and JJ opened two restaurants, The Cecil and Minton's, both occupying classic Harlem spaces rich with history. And just as people flocked to Alexander's living room where the food was plentiful, the cocktails were sweet, and the company was sweeter, the Afro-Asian-American flavor profile brought diners to a part of Harlem that many had never visited before. *Esquire* named The Cecil the best new restaurant in America and reservations became hard to come by. There were nights when ambassadors dined with world leaders and nights when there were so many Grammy Award winners at a table that no one was surpised when they burst into song. You can get roast chicken and grilled salmon anywhere, but you had to come uptown for plaintain kelewele and tofu gnocchi with black garlic crema and scallions.

As you'll see when you begin to cook from this collection, Alexander and JJ are artists first and cooks second. As they begin new creative journeys professionally, this cookbook commemorates a once-in-a-lifetime collaboration. Nobody saved the menu, or the recipes, for many Harlem's most iconic suppers during its first Renaissance when writers like Langston Hughes, Zora Neale Hurston, Claude McKay, and Jessie Fauset began to find their voices. But what

Paul Kellogg wrote about the magic and power of Harlem to inspire new and diverse voices with the power to change the world is as true now as it ever was: "We are interpreting a racial and cultural revival in the new environment of the nothern city; interpreting the affirmative genius of writers, thinkers, poets, artists, singers, and musicians, which make for a new rapprochement between races at the same time that they contribute to the common pot of civilization."

These recipes were developed by Alexander Smalls and JJ Johnson. While chef at The Cecil, JJ brought these recipes to life in the kitchen and with the cooking team. The "I" in the recipe headnotes refers to JJ, unless otherwise noted.

We hope this book will allow you to visit Harlem every time you make one of these recipes, and that you'll find, as we have, that the dishes gathered here both fill your plate and feed your imagination. To paraphrase that great Harlem Renaissance poet Jean Toomer:

Harlem is the kind of place that calls you from your home and teaches you how to dream.

Between Harlem and Heaven

AND

AFRO-ASIAN-AMERICAN COOKING FOR
BIG NIGHTS, WEEKNIGHTS, & EVERY DAY

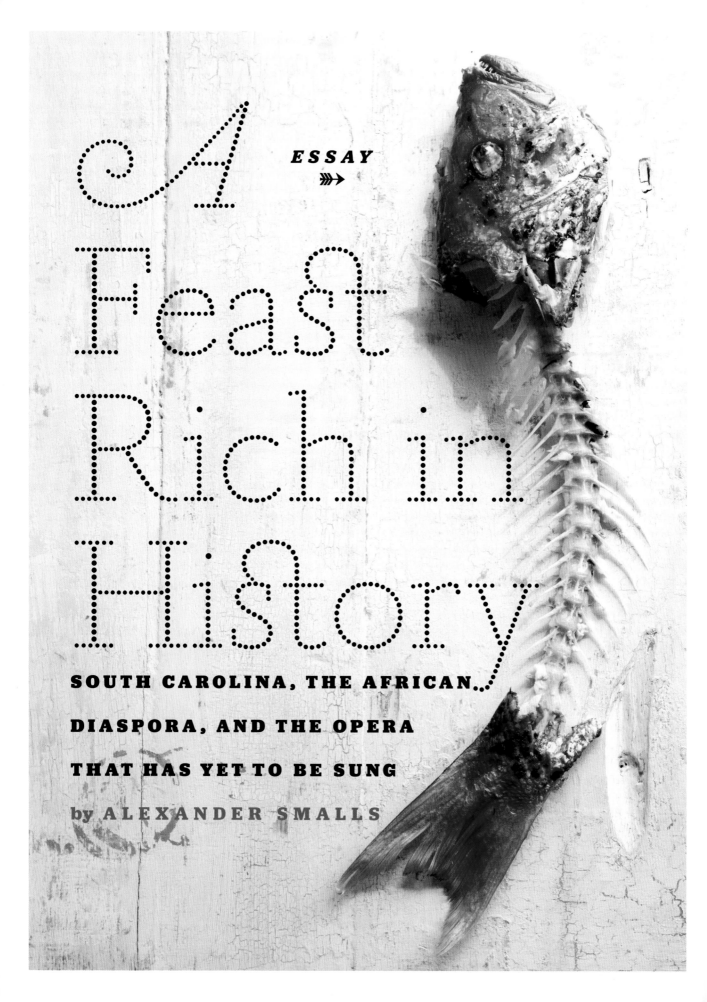

A Feast Rich in History

SOUTH CAROLINA, THE AFRICAN DIASPORA, AND THE OPERA THAT HAS YET TO BE SUNG

by ALEXANDER SMALLS

I was born and raised in Spartanburg, South Carolina—
"Upcountry" it was called. But because my father's family migrated from the Charleston, Beaufort, and Sea Island region of the state, our home was considered a "Lowcountry" household: rich in African-American culture and southern traditions. I was told it was because of the food we ate: lots of seafood stews, soups, fish, and chicken that were always spicy, and more rice than any of my friends, as often as twice a day. We sometimes even ate rice for breakfast with eggs. As a child, music, particularly singing, was my first love. A classically trained baritone, I toured the world as an opera singer, winning both a Tony and a Grammy for my recording of *Porgy and Bess* with the Houston Grand Opera in the mid-'70s and appearing on Broadway, in national and international concert halls, in opera houses, and at several music festivals.

But my love for food and entertaining always brought me back to the kitchen, driven by the memories of the dishes of my youth and the extraordinary people who cooked them. So it was no surprise to me when I opened the doors of my first New York restaurant. Cafe Beulah showcased Southern revival cooking, which was my updated version of Lowcountry cooking done at its highest level. Those years of singing abroad throughout Europe expanded my palate, and I began applying European techniques to many aspects of my heritage cooking. But the global culinary conversation around food was beginning even back then. Coastal South Carolina, particularly Charleston, was one of the biggest slave ports in the New World. That history and culture colored our daily lives. My grandfather, Ed Smalls, the son of African slaves, was a farmer and a great storyteller. It was because of him that I knew that the Lowcountry cooking of my childhood was heavily influenced by the West African slave trade. He taught me that African people were the bedrock of the agricultural revolution in the South, that they had brought with them their seeds, farming expertise, and cooking techniques.

In the process, I learned that the Asian diaspora crisscrossed the African diaspora throughout history and, most powerfully, on the plate. For example, roti—the Indian flatbread also known as chapati—was as beloved in Trinidad, Suriname, and South Africa as it was in Singapore, Sri Lanka, and Malaysia.

The Afro-Asian flavor profile that I wanted to bring to our Harlem restaurants was far from conceptual—and let's be clear, I hate the word "fusion." For the last twenty years, I've been like Matthew Henson, the great African-American explorer who made seven voyages to the North Pole with Robert Peary and became the first black to be invited to be a member of the Explorers Club. Except that where Henson went north to the Arctic region, I went south and west and east: hot on the trail of the cuisine of the African diaspora. I've traveled the world eating and studying, cooking and exploring. My goal has always been to document and share the spirit and the scholarship of Africans from China to Brazil to the Caribbean to Europe to North America and how their traditions gave us the food we eat today. That's the thrust of all of this for me. It's bigger than being a chef. It's bigger than cooking. It's really about realizing not only myself, but my race and my ancestors. It's an homage.

I've never cared much about being a celebrated chef.

For me, each restaurant I've done has been about re-creating the hospitality of my home and celebrating the African-American culinary experience at the highest levels.

In the beginning of my career as a restaurateur, I wanted to join the ranks of great food luminaries that mirrored my journey. Women like Edna Lewis, Leah Chase, and South Carolina's very own Vertamae Smart-Grosvenor really embody the elegance of our Southern foodways and its cooking. Not just a "soul food kitchen." Not fried chicken and big pots of greens. After I opened my first three restaurants, Cafe Beulah, Sweet Ophelia, and Shoebox Café, I took a ten-year hiatus and dedicated myself to travel and studying the African diaspora. So by the time it came time to open The Cecil and Minton's, the conversation for me had gotten bigger. I needed an adventurous partner, a culinary scout to assist me on my quest. Once upon a time, black people dominated the American kitchen, both in restaurants and in homes. But in the twentieth century, that changed, and it took me a long time to find a chef to join me on my journey to create this Afro-Asian food profile. I studied scores of résumés, interviewed scores of talented young people, and spent hours researching gifted young chefs of color online. Then one day, I stumbled on a video of a young chef that caught my eye: Joseph "JJ" Johnson. He was cooking grits with smothered shrimp. This was a stunning coincidence, because that dish was my dad's signature dish, the one my father made on holidays and for special Sunday mornings. It's not the kind of dish you see on television every day. JJ was quiet, focused, and determined. I knew, in an instant, that he was the winner. I had found my guy. I remember hitting mute on the television screen and silently nodding at him. "Okay, JJ. Let's cook."

When Richard Parsons, Laura Parsons, and I decided we would open a restaurant together in Harlem, our mission was very clear: We'd serve great food, play the best music, and, most importantly, strive to be good citizens in the community. We wanted to celebrate the heritage of storied people and give something back. Why come uptown, if not to be a part of the rebuilding of Harlem? This was our chance to fulfill a dream we all shared while bringing something unique to a special place. Once we found a location, we realized that the restaurant space was a heritage landmark and the hotel housed the famous Minton's Playhouse as well.

Understanding that all those extraordinary artists, writers, and musicians who once stayed in the rooms of the hotel were a part of the legacy we now served, we were proud. Like every part of opening a restaurant, we needed a great recipe: a plan and a product that

represented our intent and conviction. The first thing we did was put together an amazing design and organization team and hire the remaining creative and operations force to make it happen. We had decided to open not one but two restaurants: Minton's would have the jazz component, and The Cecil menu would feature our Afro-Asian-American flavor profile, a new culinary concept no one had ever heard of. Did I mention that we were going to open both restaurants just a month apart? It was September 2013. Years later, friends and journalists asked how I ever thought that opening two restaurants, at the same time, was a sane proposition. I always told them the same thing: "No one told me I couldn't."

We take great pride in all we've achieved and imagined. We set the table for the world, and they came: critics, bloggers, dignitaries, and celebrities flocked to taste what everyone was talking about. On any given night the room was the tasting grounds for the world to come meet, greet, and eat with us. Loyal Harlemites claim us as one of their own best inventions. Harlem welcomed us to our new home like we'd always been there. We hosted presidents, ministers, governors, mayors, and senators, movie stars, rock stars, rap and hip-hop gods, and divas. At our tables, you could find men of the cloth and men who've created celebrated fashions from cloth.

The cookbook you are holding in your hands is about digging deep into our American heritage and setting the table with simple ingredients and bold flavors, presented in an entirely new way. Whether you're serving something as simple as a our mac and cheese with rosemary and a side of our okra fries for a Meatless Monday supper, or if you're feeding a crowd with our Afro-Asian-American gumbo, we know that these are meals that are steeped with the flavors of Harlem, that one-of-a-kind uptown hospitality and grace.

The recipes in this book represent a unique culinary discipline of global taste and cooking styles, born from an extraordinary culture, skilled farming, and kitchen practices of African people who, through forced migration, traveled across five continents. The eclectic flavor profile and recipes here were created by myself and Chef Joseph "JJ" Johnson as an edible culinary conversation that celebrates and pays homage to the legacy of the African diaspora.

CUMIN, CORIANDER SEEDS, AND PINK PEPPERCORNS:

A Caribbean Childhood

by JJ JOHNSON

ESSAY ⟫→

Although I didn't understand at first what Alexander was talking about by an Afro-Asian flavor profile, by the time we opened, I understood: He was talking about the food of my childhood, the food I had eaten my whole entire life. I'd managed to graduate culinary school and cook at some of the finest restaurants in New York without ever realizing that the very mix of my family represented the African diaspora at its broadest.

I used to go in the kitchen with my Puerto Rican grandmother, and her kitchen would smell like cumin, coriander seeds, and pink peppercorns. My grandmother would play music by Latin artists like Tito Puente and Ray Barretto in the background. She made cooking fun. She would call out to me to help her: "JJ, get the rice. Grab the rice! Wash the rice." I'd have to climb on a step stool to reach the sink. I was seven years old.

She would cook up a feast of color: beets, purple yam, patty pan squash. She was an amazing cook, but I was a typical American kid. This was the Poconos in the 1980s, and we lived around the corner from my grandparents. My mom was a master of American suburban cuisine: lasagna, barbecue chicken. That was the food I loved to eat.

I would stand on a milk crate and try to help. Before too long, I was peeling carrots and onions for her and chopping celery as she cooked. She'd always have a big pot of homemade chicken stock going. My great-aunts lived with my grandmother: Tía Candy and Tía Con. All three of those women could cook. The house was always full of food. There was never a moment when you walked in and there wasn't something on the stove.

I was in the kitchen with my grandmother, Iris, every day. My mom would drop me off before she went to work and I'd spend all day in the kitchen with my grandmother. Then when I started kindergarten, I went to school for a few hours and then would go to Iris's kitchen. I remember my mom used to get upset with her: "You need to help him with his schoolwork. You should be teaching him how to write his letters, he shouldn't be cooking with you."

Food was home and home was food.

And when I first traveled to Ghana with Alexander, that also felt like home. We were invited to cook an American Thanksgiving with a team of Ghanian cooks. I had no idea what the level of their skills would be. The first day, I went into the kitchen and I handed out these prep sheets. They looked at me with raised eyebrows, but they were game. There was this kid in the corner, Miguel. He was making this dish and I went over with my pad. I said, "Miguel, what are you cooking?" He said, "I'm making piri piri sauce." I'd never heard of it. What was it? He said, "It's onions, garlic, onion powder, bird's-eye chile. We blend it." He then took that mix and rubbed it on these prawns. The prawns were larger than my hands. We roasted them in the oven. When they were done, I took one out and ate it. It was delicious, and the heat, the spice, was scathing. I started to sweat. The whole kitchen started laughing at me, but at that moment we began to relate to each other as family. Home is where the hot sauce is. I'd had the yellow from Barbados, the red from Puerto Rico, and now there was the piri piri from West Africa. "Food here, it makes you sweat," Miguel said, with a smile.

Miguel became my new homie. Every day we went to the markets and shopped for food. The flavors reminded me of the Caribbean scents and smells of my childhood. There was music playing in the background just like there was in my grandmother's kitchen. And then there it was: pasteles. I grew up on pasteles. Smashed yam or yucca. You fold it in with chicken or pork, beef or shrimp. You put it in a banana leaf and you boil it. Straight from my grandmother's kitchen. But it turns out to be a dish that comes from Ghana. Miguel and I had that dish all the time in Ghana.

I saw yams that were taller than me. Going through the fish market and grabbing fish, I was seeing fish jump right out the boat. The fish market reminded me of Japan and Hunts Point Fulton Fish Market in New York at the very same time. I saw women carrying food on their head to get home from the market, not as a postcard image, but as a way of life. Then it happened, I was standing on a street corner in Accra and I smelled a street vendor cooking a stew. There it was: cumin, coriander, and pink peppercorn. Not cumin and coriander as you might smell it in an Indian dish, but those flavors combining in a Latino way. I was back in my grandmother's kitchen in an instant; decades fell away in moments, an ocean was crossed, and I was back in the Poconos, back in time, all with one stir of that stew. The connector of everything was—is—food.

This book is a result of a culinary conversation that we're having in Harlem. It's about the food of Africa and the food of Asia and how they have met on the plate all around the world.

Don't feel like you have to read it cover to cover. Feel free to sample and scat through these recipes. We encourage you to improvise, like Charlie Parker once did in these hallowed halls of Minton's. Everything in this book tastes good with everything. Every sauce in this book will be equally delicious whether you throw it on chicken or beef, a bowl of rice or a platter of grilled vegetables. We like leftovers in Harlem, so even if there's just a little bit of, say, pork suya in the pot after dinner, don't be afraid to serve it up the next morning alongside a batch of freshly scrambled eggs. We think that you don't need another cookbook to tell you how to sear scallops or roast a chicken. This is a choose-your-own-adventure cookbook: You can follow the recipes as they're written and make one new flavorful dish after another. Or you can add our sauces, marinades, seasonings to your favorite mains and branch out just a little bit by mixing it up with our sides and salads: Maybe try a purple yam puree instead of your usual mash or try our pineapple black fried rice instead of your usual rice pilaf. Jazz consists of three elements: blues, improvisation, and swing. For so many of us, making dinner interesting is the blues: What I am to cook tonight? So you start there and then you take one of our recipes and feel free to improvise: Don't be afraid to use your favorite proteins and spices. Swing is the thing that brings it all together. It's when you're in the kitchen, blasting your favorite song, and you're just having fun. We can't write swing into the recipes. There's no way to measure it by the cup or spoonful, but I promise you that if you can add a little swing to the mix when you're making these dishes, your guests will be able to taste it. Swing is the umami of Harlem.

Salads

Grilled "Watermelon Garden" Salad *with* Lime Mango Dressing *and* Cornbread Croutons

Few things say Harlem in the summertime like fresh watermelon. In 1935, when African-American businessman George Jones opened his classic movie theater, the Harlem, he didn't just serve the usual fare of soft drinks, candy, and popcorn. In between his home (which was next door) and the theater, he opened what he called a "Watermelon Garden" with picnic tables and umbrellas where patrons could gather and socialize before and after the films.

If you've never grilled watermelon in the summertime, then you're in for a treat. Grilling caramelizes the sweetness of the fruit, and the char gives just a hint of smoky flavor. The wood flavor of the grill will come through the watermelon, but it won't be overpowering like the charred tomato or charred vegetables.

Just make sure to slice your watermelon thick enough that it doesn't fall apart while you're turning it on the grill.

Use some stale cornbread from the day before to add texture. It'll be familiar yet wholly different from anything you're used to.

6 to 8 servings

PREP TIME
20 minutes
COOKING TIME
15 minutes
TOTAL TIME
35 minutes

3 pounds seedless watermelon, peel left on, cut into 1-inch-thick slabs
olive oil
kosher salt
½ cup hulled pumpkin seeds
¼ teaspoon ground cayenne
1 teaspoon sugar
4 cups 1-inch cubes cornbread (½ of recipe on page 28, or purchased)
2 tablespoons unsalted butter, melted

8 fresh shiso leaves, shredded (or Thai basil or mint)
½ cup dates, pitted and chopped
1 serrano chile, sliced into rings
¼ cup Lime Mango Dressing (page 27)
freshly ground black pepper
½ cup ricotta or mascarpone

Heat a grill pan to medium-high heat. Drizzle the watermelon slices with just enough oil to thinly coat and place them on the hot grill.

Grill each side of the watermelon slices for about 2 minutes, until charred. Transfer to a plate and season with salt.

Remove the rind and dice the grilled watermelon into large cubes.

Preheat the oven to 350°F. Toss the pumpkin seeds with the cayenne, sugar, and 2 teaspoons oil and place on a small baking sheet. Roast for 6 to 10 minutes, until golden.

Brush the cornbread cubes with the melted butter and place in a single layer on a baking sheet. Put in the oven along with the

pumpkin seeds and bake for 10 minutes, turning halfway with a flexible spatula. Remove from the oven when the croutons are toasted and golden.

Toss the watermelon, shiso, dates, and chile in the bowl with the dressing. Taste and adjust the seasoning with salt and pepper. Add the cornbread croutons and toss very gently to combine without breaking the croutons. Spoon the salad onto a large platter and garnish with the pumpkin seeds and cheese.

LIME MANGO DRESSING

The lime in this dressing provides a sharper tang than lemon would.

Makes 1 cup

½ cup coarsely chopped ripe mango
¼ cup fresh lime juice
¼ cup dry sake
2 tablespoons champagne vinegar
1 teaspoon minced seeded bird's-eye chile
½ teaspoon kosher salt
¼ cup canola oil

Put all of the ingredients except the oil in a blender. Blend on high. After the ingredients are blended, slowly add the oil and continue to blend until the mixture is thickened and emulsified.

Makes one
8-inch square or
9-inch round

FRESH BAKED CORNBREAD

4 tablespoons unsalted butter, melted
1 cup milk
1 large egg
1¼ cups yellow cornmeal
1 cup all-purpose flour
½ cup sugar
1 tablespoon baking powder
½ teaspoon Aleppo pepper
  (or you can use ancho chile powder)
½ teaspoon salt
1 cup grated white cheddar cheese

Preheat the oven to 400°F. Brush the bottom and sides of an 8-inch square or 9-inch round cake pan with some of the melted butter.

In a large bowl, beat the remaining melted butter, milk, and egg with a fork or wire whisk until well mixed. In a separate bowl, combine the cornmeal, flour, sugar, baking powder, Aleppo pepper, and salt. Stir into the egg mixture and blend until the flour is just moistened (the batter will be lumpy). Gently fold in the cheese and set the batter aside to rest for 5 minutes.

Pour the batter into the prepared pan; use a rubber spatula to scrape batter from the bowl. Spread the batter evenly in the pan. Bake for 25 minutes, or until it is golden brown and a toothpick inserted in the center comes out clean.

Collard Green Salad *with* Coconut Dressing

4 to 6 servings

PREP TIME
8 minutes

COOKING TIME
5 minutes

TOTAL TIME
13 minutes

Every few months, some food magazine or blog pops up the same tired headline: "Are Collard Greens the New Kale?" No. Collards have worked harder than kale ever will. Collards are out there digging ditches and roofing houses while kale goes to spin class and leaves early for brunch.

Collards are natural antioxidants, rich in vitamins A, C, and K, full of fiber and low in calories. But—and this is a big one—collards have a long history of being a vegetable that people only cook the crap out of. They're braised and simmered within an inch of being edible and, well, that's got to stop.

Our friends always eat this dish and say, "Isn't this a kale salad?" The goal is to serve the greens raw so that we think of them as something healthy and delicious rather than something you combine with bacon fat and cook down.

Collards have a natural bitterness, and the elements of this recipe balance those strong flavors with sweetness and spice: sweetness in the coconut milk, spice in the smoky chipotle.

There's a brightness to the dressing that perfectly balances the bitterness of the collards and will give your guests the benefit of enjoying everything collards have to offer. To me, this dish is simplicity done well.

3 cups shredded collard greens
1 red onion, thinly sliced
1 English cucumber, peel left on, sliced into half-moon shapes
about ¼ cup Coconut Dressing (page 32)

kosher salt and freshly ground black pepper
¼ cup Adzuki Red Beans (page 188)
¼ cup candied cashews

In a large bowl, toss the greens with the onion and cucumber with just enough dressing to coat and season to taste with salt and pepper.

Top the salad with the beans and candied cashews.

COCONUT DRESSING

*Makes about
2 cups*

PREP TIME
8 minutes

COOKING TIME
5 minutes

TOTAL TIME
13 minutes

1 tablespoon cumin seeds
1 teaspoon minced fresh ginger
2 shallots, chopped
¼ cup canned chipotles in adobo
1 cup coconut milk
¼ cup fresh lime juice
¼ cup Dijon mustard
3 tablespoons champagne vinegar

Put the cumin seeds in a small dry sauté pan. Toast over medium heat until fragrant, 3 to 5 minutes.

Combine the toasted cumin seeds with the remaining ingredients in a blender and blend until smooth.

Store in a covered nonreactive container. Refrigerate for up to 3 weeks.

Daikon Radish Salad *with* Crispy Shallots, Walnuts, *and* Asian Pear Dressing

4 to 8 servings

PREP TIME
30 minutes

COOKING TIME
1 hour
30 minutes

TOTAL TIME
2 hours

I like radishes because they give a mild, peppery heat and they're consistent throughout the year. Daikon radishes are closely identified with Japan, even though they're originally from Southeast Asia, where they continue to find new uses for them. For this dish, getting the crispy shallots just right is the hardest part: You want to let them get golden brown and really, really crispy — so they can stand up to the dressing like a good onion ring can stand up to a dipping sauce. Don't neglect the shallots.

The Asian pear dressing is one of my favorites. The African nectar tea is very fruit forward and herby, a surprising but perfect base for the dressing. And of course, you can whip up a batch of the African nectar tea as a pairing drink for the salad.

1 pound daikon radish,
   peeled and thinly sliced

1 pound watermelon radishes,
   peeled and thinly sliced

3 large carrots, shaved into
   thin strips with a vegetable peeler

2 cups arugula

¾ cup pomegranate seeds
   (about ½ pomegranate)

1 recipe Poached Pears in an African
   Nectar Tea Broth (page 211)

¼ cup white wine vinegar

1 shallot, minced

1 bird's-eye chile, minced

2 teaspoons Dijon mustard

1 cup olive oil

kosher salt and
   freshly ground black pepper

¼ cup Crispy Shallots (recipe below)

1 cup Spiced Walnuts (page 34; or good
   store-bought spiced walnuts, crushed)

In a large bowl, gently toss together the radishes, carrots, arugula, and pomegranate seeds.

Combine 1 cup of the liquid from the poached pears with the vinegar, minced shallot, chile, and mustard in a blender. Blend until smooth. Slowly add the oil, continuing to blend until the dressing is thick and creamy. Season to taste with salt and pepper.

Lightly coat the salad with about ¼ cup of the blended dressing and gently toss again.

Cut the poached pears in half lengthwise and place each half flat side down on a cutting board; slice through each pear from the bottom every ¼ inch until about three quarters of the way up, so that the pear is still attached at the very top.

Fan out the sliced pears on serving plates and arrange the dressed salad next to them. Top with the shallots and walnuts.

CRISPY SHALLOTS

1 cup vegetable oil

3 large shallots, peeled
   and thinly sliced

kosher salt

Makes ½ cup

PREP TIME
5 minutes

COOKING TIME
8 minutes

TOTAL TIME
13 minutes

In a 2-quart saucepan, heat the oil to 320°F.

Carefully add the shallots and fry until light brown, about 8 minutes. Remove the shallots from the oil with a slotted spoon and place on paper towels to remove excess oil and cool. Season the shallots with salt as they start to cool.

CHEF JJ'S KITCHEN TIPS

When frying something like the crispy shallots, always make sure to season the item as soon as it comes out of the oil to drain. This ensures that the seasoning will be absorbed properly.

Makes 2 cups

SPICED WALNUTS

PREP TIME
5 minutes
COOKING TIME
35 minutes
TOTAL TIME
40 minutes

8 ounces walnuts

¼ cup sugar

¼ teaspoon ground cayenne

2 teaspoons kosher salt

1 cup vegetable oil

In a 4-quart pot, cover the walnuts with just enough water to submerge them completely and bring to a boil; boil for 10 minutes.

Drain the walnuts, put them in a bowl, and pat dry with a paper towel. Add the sugar, cayenne, and salt and toss with a large spoon to coat the nuts with the mixture.

Remove the nuts from the spiced sugar and sift off the excess mixture.

Heat the oil in a 2-quart saucepan and fry the nuts until golden brown and fragrant, about 5 minutes. Remove the walnuts from the oil with a slotted spoon and place on paper towels to drain.

Let cool for 20 minutes, then crush the walnuts in a food processor on the pulse setting or with a heavy pan.

Roasted Beet Salad *with* Apples, Figs, *and* Citrus Dressing

I love beets. Their North African roots appeal to me, of course, but this is a distinctly American dish.

I always challenge kids to a taste contest—beets versus Skittles, which ones are sweeter? The answer is beets. We get our beets from Chef's Garden in Ohio (chefs-garden.com—and they'll deliver straight to your house now). They get all these crazy colored beets: candy striped, rainbow, yellow, orange, pink. Many home cooks will be tempted to boil the beets because it's easier, but roasting gives them a deeper flavor. Reminder: Wear gloves and don't do any prep on a porous surface unless you want your kitchen to look like the set of *Dexter*.

Figs have two peak times of the year—summertime and fall. Sweet and tangy, this salad has everything you love in it.

6 servings

PREP TIME
20 minutes
COOKING TIME
1 hour
10 minutes
TOTAL TIME
1 hour
30 minutes

2 pounds baby or medium beets
3 tablespoons olive oil
¼ cup Citrus Dressing (page 37)

kosher salt and freshly ground black pepper
2 cups baby arugula
1 pint figs, quartered
1 Fuji apple, quartered and sliced

Preheat the oven to 425°F.

Trim the beets, leaving 1 inch of the stem, and coat lightly with the oil. Wrap tightly in aluminum foil and place on a baking sheet in the oven. Roast until tender and easily pierced with a knife, about 1 hour. Remove from the oven and let cool for about 10 minutes.

Peel the beets with a small, sharp knife over a piece of parchment paper to prevent staining your cutting board.

While the beets are still warm, cut each one in half and then each half into 4 to 6 wedges and put them in a large mixing bowl. While still warm, toss them with half of the dressing, 1 teaspoon salt, and ¼ teaspoon pepper. Taste for seasoning.

Add the arugula and the remaining dressing and gently toss to combine. Plate the salad and top with the figs and apples.

CITRUS DRESSING

- ¼ cup orange juice
- 1 tablespoon fresh lemon juice
- ½ teaspoon light brown sugar
- ⅛ teaspoon grated nutmeg
- 1 tablespoon chopped fresh Thai basil
- 2 teaspoons Dijon mustard
- ½ teaspoon kosher salt, or more to taste
- ¼ teaspoon freshly ground black pepper, or more to taste
- ¼ cup olive oil

Put all the ingredients except the oil in a blender and blend until completely combined. Slowly add the oil, continuing to blend until emulsified.

Season with salt and pepper to taste.

Delicata Squash Salad *with* Yuzu Buttermilk Dressing

4 to 6 servings

PREP TIME
10 minutes

COOKING TIME
45 minutes

TOTAL TIME
55 minutes

My grandmother roasted butternut squash whole. She'd do it with the skin on to add texture; otherwise it can be too mushy. She'd chop it up, then top it off with some cane syrup. This was a regular vegetable dish when I was growing up.

Delicata is a small squash that falls somewhere between acorn squash and butternut. It disappeared almost entirely from menus in the 1940s because of growing problems, but it was brought back in the 2000s thanks to researchers at Cornell.

2 delicata squashes
   (about 10 ounces each), halved
   lengthwise, seeded, and
   cut into ½-inch half moons
2 tablespoons olive oil
½ teaspoon kosher salt
½ teaspoon freshly ground
   black pepper

5 heads baby bok choy,
   sliced into 1-inch strips
about ¼ cup Yuzu Buttermilk Dressing
   (page 39)
¼ cup Pickled Red Onions (page 201)

Preheat the oven to 425°F.

In a large bowl, gently toss the squash with the oil, salt, and pepper. Roast the squash on a large baking sheet, turning occasionally, until tender and golden, 35 to 40 minutes. Set aside to cool.

Once the squash is cool to the touch, toss together in a large bowl with the sliced bok choy and enough dressing to coat.

Top with the pickled onions and serve.

CHEF JJ'S KITCHEN TIPS

There's no need to peel delicata squash. The pale yellow and green skin gives great contrasting texture to its creamy flesh once cooked.

YUZU BUTTERMILK DRESSING

Makes ²/₃ cups

- ½ cup mayonnaise
- ½ cup buttermilk
- ¾ cup bottled yuzu juice
- kosher salt and ground white pepper

Whisk together the mayonnaise, buttermilk, and yuzu in a large bowl until smooth.

Season to taste with salt and white pepper.

"Are Collard Greens the New Kale?" No. Collards have worked harder than kale ever will. Collards are out there digging ditches and roofing houses while kale goes to spin class and leaves early for brunch.

Harlem Market Salad

Spinach and Black Lentil Salad with Shiitake Mushrooms and Citrus Ginger Soy Dressing

This is a great farmers' market salad that you can change up in a dozen different ways. If you're on your way home from work and make a quick stop at a market, you can pick up spinach, red onion, shiitakes, and an orange for under $10. Grab some black lentils from your pantry and less than an hour later, you'll have this filling, elegant meal.

The three key ingredients are a leafy green veg, citrus, and a vegetable that adds that umami flavor. So if you don't like spinach, try chicory. Switch out the shiitake mushrooms for butternut squash. Instead of orange segments, try grapefruit. You really can't get this wrong.

The secret to this salad is the citrus ginger soy dressing. It's our version of that dressing you get at a Japanese restaurant that you want to put on everything.

4 to 6 servings

PREP TIME
15 minutes
COOKING TIME
30 minutes
TOTAL TIME
45 minutes

Save the stems removed from the shiitake mushrooms. Freeze them, stored in an airtight freezer bag, and use them in the next vegetable stock you make. They will add a rich and earthy essence to your recipe bases.

CHEF JJ'S
KITCHEN
TIPS

¾ cup beluga or French lentils, picked over for stones
1 teaspoon garlic powder
1 teaspoon onion powder
1 bird's-eye chile, seeded and minced, or ½ teaspoon red chile flakes
8 ounces shiitake mushrooms, cleaned and stems removed (about 4 cups)

2 tablespoons olive oil
kosher salt and freshly ground black pepper
3 cups baby spinach
about ¼ cup Citrus Ginger Soy Dressing (page 44), plus more for serving
1 cup orange supremes (from 2 oranges)
1 shallot, thinly sliced

In a 4-quart pot, combine the lentils, garlic powder, onion powder, chile, and enough water to cover by 2 inches.

Bring to a boil over high heat. Reduce the heat and simmer,

uncovered, until the lentils are tender but firm and still hold their shape, about 30 minutes. Remove from the heat and drain the lentils, discarding the cooking liquid.

While the lentils are simmering, preheat the oven to 350°F.

Toss the mushrooms in a bowl with the oil and salt and pepper to taste, making sure to coat them evenly.

Transfer to a foil-lined baking sheet and roast until tender and browned, about 20 minutes.

In a large bowl, toss the spinach, warm lentils, and mushrooms gently together with the dressing (enough to coat the salad lightly) until the spinach is just wilted. Season to taste with salt and pepper. Arrange the salad on a platter and top with the oranges and shallot. Serve with additional dressing alongside.

CITRUS GINGER SOY DRESSING

Makes ¾ cup

- ¼ cup orange juice
- 1 tablespoon fresh lemon juice
- 1 teaspoon Dijon mustard
- 1 small shallot, minced
- 1 teaspoon minced ginger
- ½ cup soy sauce
- ⅓ cup vegetable oil
- kosher salt and freshly ground pepper

Combine the citrus juices, mustard, shallots, ginger, and soy sauce in a blender. Blend on a low setting and slowly pour in oil until the dressing becomes smooth and thick. Season to taste.

Store in a covered nonreactive container. Refrigerate for up to 3 weeks.

Grilled Ahi Tuna *with* Noodle Salad *and* Yuzu Turmeric Dressing

hen you're trying to eat healthier—say, the day after you've thrown down on a giant platter of our Dibi Short Ribs (page 68), just the word "salad" can be a drag. We made this recipe for days when you want to eat healthy but you want something more inspiring than the prepackaged salad you might pick up at your local grocery store. The tuna can be done in a grill pan in minutes. And the buckwheat noodles have a low glycemic index, but with the citrusy, spicy dressing, they feel like a treat.

4 servings

PREP TIME
15 minutes

COOKING TIME
10 minutes

TOTAL TIME
25 minutes

1 red or yellow bell pepper, julienned
½ small head Savoy cabbage, shredded (about 6 cups)
½ cup Pickled Red Onions (page 201)
Yuzu Turmeric Dressing (page 47)

4 (5-ounce) tuna steaks
3 tablespoons olive oil
kosher salt and freshly ground black pepper
6 ounces buckwheat noodles, cooked according to package directions, rinsed under cold water, and drained

In a large bowl, toss together the bell peppers, cabbage, and pickled onions. Add the dressing and toss to coat. Set aside.

Heat a grill to medium-high heat. Brush the tuna with the oil and season with salt and pepper, then grill, turning over once, until browned on the outside but still pink in the center, 6 to 8 minutes total.

Let the tuna stand for 3 minutes. Slice across the grain, then plate over the buckwheat noodles and top with cabbage salad.

YUZU TURMERIC DRESSING

- 4 tablespoons vegetable oil
- 1 shallot, thinly sliced
- 1 teaspoon minced fresh ginger
- 1 teaspoon ground turmeric
- 2 tablespoons bottled yuzu juice
- kosher salt and freshly ground black pepper

Makes ⅓ cup

PREP TIME
5 minutes
COOKING TIME
10 minutes
TOTAL TIME
15 minutes

Heat 1 tablespoon of the oil in a small saucepan over medium heat. Add the shallot and ginger and cook, stirring, until the shallot is softened, about 3 minutes.

Add the turmeric and toast in the oil until aromatic, about 1 minute. Whisk in the yuzu, scraping up the turmeric from the bottom of the pan, and then whisk in the remaining 3 tablespoons oil. Bring to a simmer and gently simmer until the mixture looks creamy, about 2 minutes.

Season with salt and pepper to taste and chill. Store in a nonreactive airtight container in the refrigerator for up to 5 days.

Grilled Octopus Salad

O ctopus can be an intimidating dish to cook at home. The key is to ask your local seafood counter to clean it before they wrap it up. We love this paired with our Spicy Black-Eyed Peas (page 195) and Carrot Curry Puree (page 162). Plated together, these three sides make a rich, filling, colorful platter of good stuff.

4 cups orange juice

2 limes, halved

1½ lemons, halved

1 orange, halved

2 cups white wine

4 sprigs fresh thyme

2 bay leaves

4 carrots, cut into 4 pieces each

2 onions, quartered

3 celery stalks, cut into 4 pieces each

2 tablespoons whole black peppercorns

2 pounds octopus, cleaned

2 tablespoons olive oil

kosher salt and freshly ground black pepper

2 cups watercress

3 tablespoons fresh lemon juice

4 servings

PREP TIME
10 minutes

COOKING TIME
1 hour
10 minutes

TOTAL TIME
1 hour
20 minutes

In a 6-quart pot, combine the orange juice, citrus fruits (squeezing in the juice before adding the fruits to the pot), wine, thyme, bay leaves, carrots, onions, celery, and peppercorns and bring to a boil over medium-high heat.

Once boiling, add the octopus and lower the heat to a simmer. Add water if needed to cover the octopus. Cover the pot with a tight-fitting lid and simmer for 1 hour, or until the octopus lacks resistance when pierced with the tip of a sharp knife. You can also cut off and bite into a small piece of the octopus to test its firmness. It should be tender but still have a springy bite to it.

Preheat a large cast-iron grill pan over high heat.

Remove the octopus from the liquid and cut it into large serving pieces, brush them with half of the oil, and sprinkle with salt and pepper. Grill quickly until the outside browns but the inside is not dried out, about 2 minutes per side.

Quickly toss the watercress with the remaining oil and the lemon juice. Season with salt and pepper.

Plate the grilled octopus and top with watercress salad for a great contrast of textures and flavors.

Heirloom Tomato Salad

I n a perfect world, perfect tomatoes would be available twelve months a year. But it's not perfect here in the United States, so you need to take advantage of August and September, planning every tomato dish like a delicious invasion. Step one: Find a good place to buy real heirloom tomatoes. I often have this flashback of being in Ghana at the first market there I ever went to. I remember thinking, "This tomato looks like it's an heirloom tomato." It was the same seed varietals that we see in heirlooms in the U.S. You could see it in the shape, the texture, the color, and the sizes. These were beautiful red, green, and orange tomatoes that they were selling for twenty-five cents. You'll pay ten times that in the United States.

Thinking back to that market, I wanted to figure out how to highlight this tomato salad like you might have in Ghana.

6 servings

PREP TIME
5 minutes

TOTAL TIME
20 minutes

2 pounds colorful heirloom
  tomatoes, halved, or quartered if large
¼ cup fresh Thai basil torn, plus small
  whole leaves for garnish
1 teaspoon smoked sea salt, or
  1½ teaspoons kosher salt

½ teaspoon freshly ground
  black pepper
Curry Lime Yogurt Dressing
  (recipe below)
½ cup Pickled Red Onions (page 201)

In a medium bowl, gently toss the tomatoes and basil with the salt and pepper. Let stand for 10 minutes.

Spread the dressing on a serving platter and top with the tomato salad. Garnish with pickled onions and basil leaves for an extra pop of color and flavor.

Makes ½ cup

CURRY LIME YOGURT DRESSING

½ cup full-fat Greek yogurt
1 tablespoon olive oil
1 teaspoon curry powder
1 teaspoon fresh lime juice
¼ teaspoon kosher salt, or to taste
¼ teaspoon freshly ground black pepper, or to taste

Whisk together the yogurt, oil, curry powder, and lime juice in a medium bowl until the yogurt is completely smooth and the golden color of the curry powder is evenly distributed.

Season to taste with salt and pepper. Chill until ready to use.

flavors

upon

flavors

upon

flavors

ESSAY

by JJ JOHNSON

T he food we created for The Cecil and Minton's, and the recipes in this book, are inspired by an Afro-Asian-American flavor profile: a foodway that reflects the depth and breadth of the African diaspora. It's a new concept, and if you're not into culinary history, it can be a bit of a head-scratcher. I think the simplest way to put it is that the recipes in this book are a modern take on heritage food. If you grew up in or spent significant time in the West Indies or in China or in Korea, if you're from Ghana or ever lived in Senegal or South Africa or on the coast of Costa Rica, then this food will remind you of food you ate in those places. I love it when we have guests at the restaurant say, "What did you put in this *feijoada*? It tastes just like my grand-mother's. Soooo good, but just a little different." The truth is that people aren't used to getting that super-impact flavor from food in a fine dining setting. They're used to getting strong flavors at home or in that little ethnic hidden-gem hole-in-the-wall spot. I love the way the dishes in this cookbook bridge that gap between restaurants and heritage food.

This is Heritage Food.
The biggest compliment
you can give us is that
a dish tastes like
your grandmother's.

All across America, heritage food is experiencing a renaissance. It brings together everything we've developed a passion for: sus-tainability, farm to table, eating local, thinking global. It's the kind of food you once could expect to eat only in someone's home. But now you can go out to a nice restaurant and eat gumbo and corn-bread with a great bottle of wine. Chefs now want to cook like their grandmothers. We want to cook heritage food, serve it at the highest level. We want to add our touch, make the dish look pretty, and have it taste amazing with the soul of our grandmothers in it.

I try not to give you something you've seen before. I've cooked in Ghana and Israel, down South and in Singapore. I grew up in an African diaspora household *and* I have this formal culinary education. So I look to create dishes that express who I am at a really high level. You take a bite, and you have sweet and tangy and crunchy and sour—ingredients you may recognize on a menu but haven't had together like this before.

I start with the question "How can I make this fun?" So I put the oxtail meat that I grew up eating in a dumpling wrapper. Then I serve the oxtail dumplings in a bowl with a beautiful green apple curry. I'm like a DJ who loves the mash-up: egg rolls filled with barbecue brisket and edamame, udon noodles with goat meat and West African peanut sauce, roast fish with hominy stew and homemade kimchi. Flavors upon flavors upon flavors.

NOT JUST
RISOTTO WITH PEAS

At the Culinary Institute of America, I learned the foundations: Italian cooking, French cooking, and, partly because of the popularity of Spanish chefs like Ferran Adrià, a little bit about cooking from Spain. I think we did one week of Chinese cooking. I didn't learn about the rich Lowcountry

cooking tradition that Alexander brought to life at Cafe Beulah. I didn't learn about the food of New Orleans or all that a great chef like Leah Chase has contributed to the American culinary tradition. Leah's restaurant, Dooky Chase's, was a gathering place for the Civil Rights movement in the 1960s and is still regarded today as the standard-bearer for Creole cuisine in that city.

I remember being in the second or third grade and telling my mother, "I want to be a chef." She would say, "No, you should be a politician. You should be a doctor. You should be a lawyer." You know moms. They want the best for you. But maybe if she'd known about someone like Leah Chase, she might have thought a little bit differently about the place I could occupy in the food world.

Culinary school did not do much to help me feel like I could use my history to create great food. I used to call culinary school the food factory. We all dressed the same, we talked the same, we did everything the same. We cooked celery and onions the same. We roasted chicken in the exact same way. There was no thinking outside the box. We were learning the foundations. And I get it, that's important: You have to have a foundation. But I didn't see myself in the food. I didn't know if I ever would.

We talk a lot in the restaurant world about the Indian spice traders and their legacy. But everybody misses that the spice traders came through West Africa and then crisscrossed back through the West Indies— that's why it's called the West Indies! When I started to read about all of this, I thought,

"Hold on, I'm connected to this personally." My grandfather is from Barbados. I used to go to the island as a kid. Plantain, roti, curry: These are the foods that I used to eat and now I'm reading about them, as research, for my job, in the encyclopedia. Not only could I draw a line from Barbados to West Africa to India through the spice trade, I could place myself and my family, my own personal history, on that continuum. That was exciting—and inspiring.

When Alexander approached me about cooking with him in Harlem, I was excited about the opportunity to draw on American history to change the landscape of American cuisine. That's why I'm so excited about this cookbook. If you're at all like me or my friends, you don't need another cookbook full of recipes for things like risotto and peas. You want to try familiar ingredients cooked in a different way. You want to try new flavors, new spices, new grains, and new cuts of meat.

The recipes in this book embrace all the senses. We're not just focused on look and taste; these are aromatic dishes that you can smell as they approach the table, vividly colored ingredients presented in an array of textures. This comes from our African roots. In West Africa, in particular, people like to smell their food before it comes to the table. If I could have made every page in this book scratch and sniff, I would have! Just turn to page 58, look at the picture, and then close your eyes and imagine. That cinnamon-scented guinea hen has been on the menu since our earliest days, and if we ever took it off the menu, our regulars would

revolt. I think this will become one of your favorite dishes too: something you break out for Sunday suppers and special gatherings, the kind of dish that greets your guests from the minute they open the door.

In cooking school, we were taught the five French "mother sauces" as defined by the twentieth-century master of French cooking, Auguste Escoffier: béchamel, velouté, sauce espagnole (a simple brown sauce), sauce tomate, and hollandaise. The foundational sauce to the Afro-Asian flavor profile is what we call the Mother Africa sauce: West African peanut sauce (page 56). I'd like to urge you to stop reading this book and whip up a batch of it right now.

This is a sauce that tastes good on everything.

You can pour it over a bowl of rice. You can dice up a sweet potato and mix it in as a stew. It tastes delicious with the meat of the chicken thigh crumbled into the mix. This sauce will keep for five days in the fridge and you can eat it every day, in a different way. It's an easy back-pocket sauce that you can't mess up. It's both comfort food and comforting to cook. So give it a try.

The Mother Africa Sauce

Makes about
4 cups

PREP TIME
15 minutes

COOKING TIME
1 hour

TOTAL TIME
1 hour
15 minutes

1 tablespoon olive oil

½ teaspoon cumin seeds

½ white onion, diced

½ cup coarsely chopped carrots (1 medium carrot)

1 plum tomato, chopped

¼ cup finely diced celery (1 rib)

1 clove garlic, minced (1 teaspoon)

1 bay leaf

¼ cup chopped fresh cilantro

1 bird's-eye chile, seeded and minced (1 teaspoon)

1 teaspoon kosher salt, plus more to taste

2 tablespoons fresh lemon juice (from 1 lemon)

2 tablespoons tomato paste

1 cup unsweetened, creamy peanut butter

4 cups vegetable stock

Heat the oil in a 4-quart pot over medium heat, add the cumin, and fry for 1 minute, stirring constantly. The cumin will become very aromatic and a few shades darker.

Add the onion, carrots, tomato, celery, garlic, bay leaf, cilantro, chile, salt, and lemon juice, stirring to coat the vegetables in the toasted cumin oil. Sauté until the vegetables soften, about 5 minutes.

Stir in the tomato paste and cook for 2 minutes. Once the tomato paste is incorporated, add the peanut butter, working it into the vegetables with a little stock, if needed. Cook until the oil separates from the peanut butter, about 5 minutes.

Add the stock and stir, making sure to bring up all of the tomato paste and peanut butter from the bottom of the pot so it is well blended. Increase the heat to medium-high to bring the sauce to a simmer. Cook, stirring, for 45 minutes.

Remove the bay leaf. Using an immersion blender, puree the sauce in the pot until smooth. Season with salt to taste.

Meat & Poultry

Cinnamon-Scented Fried Guinea Hen

C innamon is my favorite ingredient, and this is a dish that I'm always proud to serve. The guinea hen is very West African, while the cinnamon brings in the spice palette you might taste in a dish like Vietnamese pho. The aromatic feel of the cinnamon is the highlight of the dish. The way it smells. The way it tastes. You begin to enjoy the dish before you even take a bite. There's that highlighting moment. Serve with Charred Okra, Adzuki Red Beans, and Roasted Sweet Potatoes (pages 185, 188, and 186).

6 servings

PREP TIME
20 minutes

COOKING TIME
30 minutes

BRINING TIME
8 hours

COOLING TIME
1 hour

TOTAL TIME
10 hours

FOR BRINING:

3 bay leaves
3 bird's-eye chiles
½ cup palm sugar (you can substitute
   dark brown or cane sugar)
½ bunch fresh thyme
1 cup kosher salt
4 cinnamon sticks
1 tablespoon ground cinnamon

2 (2½-pound) Guinea hens, or
   1 (4½- to 5-pound) chicken, halved

FOR FRYING:

Vegetable oil
2 cups all-purpose flour
¼ cup ground cinnamon

BRINING

In an 8-quart stainless-steel pot, combine the bay leaves, chiles, palm sugar, thyme, salt, cinnamon sticks, and ground cinnamon with 1 gallon water and bring to a boil. Make sure to stir well so the salt is properly dissolved.

Boil for 10 minutes, then remove from the heat and let the brine cool completely.

Add the hens to the cooled brine, cover with a lid, and place in refrigerator. Let the hens brine for 8 to 12 hours.When you're ready to prepare the hens, remove them from the brine, rinse carefully under fresh cool water, and thoroughly pat dry the skin and inside cavity.

FRYING

Heat oil to 350°F in a large, deep cast-iron pan or Dutch oven, filled halfway, over medium-high heat.

Sift together the flour and cinnamon in a large flat container. Place the hens in the seasoned flour, coating evenly. Shake off excess flour and, using tongs, carefully submerge the guinea hens in the hot oil. Fry, turning every 3 minutes, until cooked through, golden brown, and crispy, about 20 minutes for hens and 25 to 30 minutes for half chickens. Remove from the oil and allow the excess oil to drain off on a paper towel–covered plate.

CHEF JJ'S KITCHEN TIPS

If you don't have a vessel deep enough to fry the whole hen you can cut the Guinea hens in half, leaving the breast, leg, and thigh connected.

Afro-Asian-American Gumbo

This gumbo dish is another story of migration and change. It starts in Senegal and then moves on to South Carolina and Louisiana before coming up to Harlem. The roux is at the heart of every good gumbo, and ours uses dried shrimp, which is a touch of Senegal. The shrimp gives it an oceany umami flavor that you wouldn't traditionally get in a Southern gumbo or a Louisiana gumbo. Louisiana comes out in the richness of the roux as you add spices. But unlike Louisiana gumbo, this dish is more about the soup than the rice, so we pour it on top of the rice like you would in South Carolina.

4 to 6 servings

PREP TIME
20 minutes
COOKING TIME
1 hour
25 minutes
TOTAL TIME
1 hour
45 minutes

4 tablespoons salted butter
¼ cup vegetable oil
½ cup all-purpose flour
1 cup minced onion
4 cloves garlic, minced
¼ cup minced celery
½ cup minced red bell pepper
½ cup grape tomatoes, halved
½ cup whole dried shrimp
¾ cup Gumbo Spice Mix (page 64)
1 tablespoon tomato paste

5 cups chicken stock
1 cup okra cut into rounds
2 tablespoons fresh lemon juice
2 teaspoons Worcestershire sauce
½ cup Chinese chicken sausage
½ cup lump crabmeat
1 cup whole fresh Gulf shrimp
kosher salt and freshly ground black
   pepper
4 cups cooked jasmine rice

In a heavy 4- to 5-quart pot, heat the butter and oil over medium heat. Once the butter begins to bubble slightly, add the flour and stir with a wooden spoon to form a smooth paste.

Cook the mixture for about 10 minutes to make a chocolate-colored roux. While the roux cooks, make sure to stir continuously, scraping the bottom and sides of the pot to avoid burning. It is important to keep a very close eye on the roux during this step. The roux can go from a complex nutty color and aroma to burnt beyond repair in a matter of minutes.

After the roux turns from a smooth peanut butter color and consistency to one resembling rich chocolate, add the onion, garlic, celery, bell pepper, and tomatoes; this will stop the roux from overcooking and burning.

Lower the heat and cook the vegetables over medium heat for 10 minutes. Add the dried shrimp, spice mix, and tomato paste and cook for 5 minutes.

Slowly whisk in the stock and stir until the stock is completely blended with the roux and vegetable mixture. Add the okra, lemon juice, Worcestershire sauce, sausage, crabmeat, and shrimp and let simmer for about 1 hour over very low heat, stirring occasionally with the wooden spoon.

Season the gumbo to taste with salt and pepper and serve over the rice.

CHEF JJ'S KITCHEN TIPS

The roux is at the heart of every delicious gumbo made. It is important to not rush the roux making process. Watch it closely and let the flavors develop at the proper time.

Makes about ⅔ cup

GUMBO SPICE MIX

- 1 tablespoon dried oregano
- 1 tablespoon dried thyme
- 1 teaspoon powdered bay leaf
- 1½ tablespoons garlic powder
- 1 tablespoon onion powder
- ½ teaspoon red chile flakes, or more to taste
- ½ teaspoon ground cayenne, or more to taste
- 2 tablespoons sugar
- 2 tablespoons smoked paprika
- 1 tablespoon kosher salt
- ½ teaspoon freshly ground black pepper

Stir together and store in an airtight container for up to 1 week.

Grilled Chicken Thighs *with* Adobo Sauce

When we started digging into Afro-Peruvian culture, we were really thrilled to start playing with Peruvian-style adobo sauce. Adobos vary widely in style. This recipe features the unexpected sweetness of rice vinegar along with West African palm sugar, which I love for its rich, caramel flavor. But you can use dark brown sugar in this recipe and your guests will love it all the same.

2 tablespoons olive oil
1 cup diced yellow onion
kosher salt
2 tablespoons minced garlic
1 teaspoon minced fresh ginger
3 bird's-eye chiles, seeded and chopped
½ cup palm sugar
    (or you can use dark brown sugar)
3 tablespoons tomato paste

1 (14.5-ounce) can stewed tomatoes
½ cup rice wine vinegar
1 cup soy sauce
3 cups chicken stock
2 bay leaves
1 teaspoon whole cloves
1 tablespoon whole black peppercorns
2 pounds boneless, skinless chicken
    thighs (about 8 thighs)

In a 4-quart pot, heat the oil over medium-high heat. When the oil is hot and begins to shimmer, add the onion and sprinkle with salt. Sauté the onion for 3 to 5 minutes, then add the garlic, ginger, and chiles and cook for 2 additional minutes.

Stir in the palm sugar and allow it to dissolve and melt down slightly, then blend in the tomato paste. Once the sugar and tomato paste are incorporated and begin to caramelize slightly, pour in the stewed tomatoes and cook for 5 minutes. Add the vinegar, soy sauce, stock, bay leaves, cloves, and peppercorns. Bring the sauce to a simmer and let cook until reduced by half, about 30 minutes. Taste and season the sauce before straining through a medium-mesh sieve; discard the solids. Let the sauce cool completely.

Place the chicken in a medium bowl and add half of the cooled

4 to 6 servings

PREP TIME
15 minutes
COOKING TIME
1 hour
TOTAL TIME
*1 hour
15 minutes*

adobo sauce. Reserve the remaining sauce for serving. Fold in the chicken to coat it with the sauce.

Preheat a cast-iron grill pan over medium heat. When the grill pan is hot, lift the chicken from the sauce, allowing excess sauce to drip back into the bowl. Place the chicken on the grill, smooth side down. Cook until the chicken is marked and releases from the grill ridges easily. Turn the chicken over and lower the heat to medium-low.

Continue to cook the chicken over medium-low heat, turning occasionally and brushing with more of the adobo sauce from the bowl to continue layering the flavor. Cook until the chicken is lightly charred and cooked through, 15 to 18 minutes. Discard any remaining adobo sauce that has been used as marinade.

Transfer the chicken to a clean work surface and let rest for 5 minutes. Serve with the reserved sauce and black rice.

Dibi Short Ribs
with Peanut Puree

4 to 6 servings

PREP TIME
10 minutes

COOKING TIME
*2 hours
(including
Peanut Puree)*

TOTAL TIME
*2 hours
10 minutes*

I f you've been to Senegal, then you've had dibi. It's a grilled meat, usually lamb, that's cut up, mixed with mustard and onions, and served wrapped in butcher paper by street vendors all over the country. It always struck me how much dibi was like the Senegalese fish and chips. So when it came time to make our own version, I wanted to play with the idea of this incredibly flavor-forward dish that you could eat with your hands but had that same mustardy deliciousness. This dibi is grilled short ribs, flavored with whole grain mustard and chile with a little maple syrup to cut the heat. Instead of bread or fries, I like to cook up Beer-Battered Long Beans (page 181) for that same crunchy satisfaction you get when you eat fish and chips. Save this recipe for the friends you never see enough of: Once they have it, they'll be clamoring for more.

2 cups beef broth
¼ cup maple syrup
2 tablespoons olive oil
1 cup sliced white onion (½ onion)
kosher salt
2 bird's-eye chiles, seeded
  and julienned

½ cup chopped green olives
2 tablespoons whole grain mustard
2 pounds beef short ribs
freshly ground black pepper
¼ cup Peanut Puree (page 70)

In a 2-quart saucepan, whisk together the broth and maple syrup to combine thoroughly and simmer over medium heat until the sauce reduces by one quarter, about 15 minutes.

While the glaze cooks, heat the oil in a large cast-iron pan over medium-high heat. When the oil is shimmering, add the onion and sprinkle with salt. Sauté for 3 to 5 minutes, until the onion begins to brown slightly. Add the chiles and olives and cook for 2 more minutes. Lower the heat and stir in the mustard. Remove the onion from the pan and set aside. Wipe out the pan.

Preheat the oven to 400°F. Season the short ribs generously with salt and pepper. Return the skillet to medium-high heat. Lay the short ribs in the pan, bone side up. Sear without moving for

2 minutes. Flip them onto one of their meaty sides and sear for 1 minute. Flip and sear the other meaty side for 1 minute. Finally, turn the ribs so they are sitting in the pan bone side down and slide the pan into the oven. Roast the short ribs to desired doneness, about 12 minutes for medium. Remove from the oven, transfer to a platter, and let rest for 10 minutes.

Carefully pour off the drippings from the skillet. Return the skillet to medium heat and add the maple syrup reduction to the pan, scraping the bottom of the pan to loosen any fond. Return the rested short ribs to the skillet, bone side down, and begin basting them with the simmering liquid. Continue basting them until the liquid reduces to a glaze and the short ribs are shiny and glazed. Transfer the ribs to a platter and top with the glaze.

Serve with the mustard onion and the peanut puree, and alongside Beer-Battered Long Beans (page 181).

Makes 1½ cups	# PEANUT PUREE

PREP TIME	1 cup raw unsalted peanuts
5 minutes	4 cups water
COOKING TIME	½ teaspoon kosher salt, to taste
2 hours	
TOTAL TIME	
2 hours	
5 minutes	

Boil the peanuts and water in a 2-quart sauce pot until the peanuts are soft and pliable, about 2 hours.

When the peanuts are soft enough to smash easily, strain from the water (reserving about ¼ of the liquid) and puree in a blender with the salt until smooth. Add a few tablespoons of the boiling liquid as needed to make a smooth and creamy puree, but make sure it's not too runny. Add the salt to taste.

Regrigerate in a covered nonreactive container for up to 2 weeks.

Bebop Chicken Chili

Fans of the great Charlie Parker know that great chili is synonymous with the birth of bebop. It was during a 1939 jam session at Dan Wall's Chili House in Harlem that Parker hit the upper chord improvisation that many credit as the lightning bolt moment that became bebop.

In honor of Charlie "Yardbird" Parker, we make our chili with chicken. It's a great game-day meal for a crowd, but it also works great as a family meal for kids. Alexander likes this on top of our Yard Dog (page 83). The secret is the Spicy Black Beans (page 98), which get their nice rich flavor from the oxtail braising liquid.

If you don't have time to do the oxtail braising liquid (page 84), you can amp up the flavors in a good beef broth by letting it simmer for an hour with cinnamon sticks, orange juice, and cilantro stems. Use ¼ cup orange juice for every quart of beef broth.

Makes 2 quarts; 4 to 6 main-course servings

PREP TIME
15 minutes
COOKING TIME
1 hour
TOTAL TIME
1 hour 15 minutes

1 tablespoon olive oil
1 large onion, diced
2 teaspoons kosher salt, or more to taste
2 tablespoons minced garlic
2 red bell peppers, diced
1 poblano pepper, diced
1½ pounds ground chicken
¼ teaspoon ground cayenne
½ teaspoon chili powder
½ teaspoon garlic powder
½ teaspoon onion powder
1 teaspoon dried oregano
1 teaspoon dried thyme
1½ cups Spicy Black Beans (page 96); or 1 (15-ounce) can black beans, rinsed and drained
2 tablespoons dark brown sugar
1 bay leaf
2 teaspoons Worcestershire sauce
1 (14.5-ounce) can stewed tomatoes
2 cups chicken stock
½ teaspoon freshly ground black pepper, or more to taste

Heat the oil over medium-high heat in a large Dutch oven and add the onion when the oil begins to shimmer. Sprinkle with ½ teaspoon of the salt and sauté for about 3 minutes, until the onion is translucent. Add the garlic, bell peppers, and poblano and cook until softened, about 5 minutes.

Once the vegetables are soft, add the chicken and spread it

out in an even layer on the bottom of the pot. Stir to crumble the chicken as it cooks.

Once the chicken begins to turn opaque, after about 3 minutes, add the spices, herbs, and the remaining 1½ teaspoons salt. Stir to coat and toast the spices and cook for about 3 minutes.

Stir in the remaining ingredients and bring to a simmer. Lower the heat to medium and cover the pot. Simmer the chili to let the flavors meld and the sauce thicken, about 45 minutes. Stir occasionally to make sure the bottom doesn't burn.

Season to taste. Let cool and store in an airtight nonreactive container in the refrigerator for up to 3 days, if you're not serving it immediately.

CHEF JJ'S
KITCHEN
TIPS

Some dishes taste better the next day. Making and storing the chili a day in advance gives the flavors a chance to meld and blend together to develop a more complex quality.

Grilled Ribeye *with* West African Black Pepper Sauce

Some people think it's terrible to put anything on a well-cooked ribeye, but this sauce is special and worth it. In West Africa, pepper sauce is the equivalent of ketchup or Tabasco. It's on the table everywhere you go: It's a tomatoey hot sauce made with Scotch bonnet or habanero peppers. At the restaurant, we do a mustardy black pepper sauce: less heat, more tang. It's delicious.

8 servings

PREP TIME
10 minutes
COOKING TIME
30 minutes
TOTAL TIME
40 minutes

4 (1½-inch-thick) bone-in ribeye steaks
   (about 1½ pounds each)
vegetable oil
kosher salt and freshly ground black
   pepper
2 cups Black Pepper Sauce
   (page 76)

Let the steaks stand at room temperature for 1 hour before cooking.

Preheat a large cast-iron grill pan over high heat. Rub the steaks with oil and season with salt and pepper on both sides. When the grill pan is smoking hot, place the steaks in the pan, making sure to not overcrowd it.

Grill the steaks, turning frequently and pressing the edges and bone into the hot pan to sear them, for 12 to 15 minutes for medium-rare, or longer if desired. Remove the steaks and let them rest for at least 10 minutes before serving.

Serve with Black Pepper Sauce.

Thoroughly pat your steaks dry before oiling and seasoning.

CHEF JJ'S
KITCHEN
TIPS

Makes 2 cups

BLACK PEPPER SAUCE

PREP TIME
5 minutes
COOKING TIME
35 minutes
TOTAL TIME
40 minutes

2 tablespoons unsalted butter, cubed
2 shallots, sliced
kosher salt
1 teaspoon fresh thyme
1 tablespoon Dijon mustard
⅓ cup brandy
2 tablespoons jarred green peppercorns (optional)
¼ cup whole black peppercorns, soaked in 1 cup water overnight, drained
1½ cups veal or low-sodium beef stock
¾ cup heavy cream
freshly ground black pepper

In a 2-quart saucepan, melt one cube of butter over medium heat. Stir in the shallots and sprinkle with salt. Cook until the shallots become translucent, about 5 minutes, then add the thyme and mustard.

Cook for about 3 minutes, then pour in the brandy to deglaze the pan. Let the sauce simmer and reduce by one quarter, about 5 minutes.

Add the peppercorns and stock and bring back to a simmer. Once the sauce has reduced by half, about 15 minutes, stir in the cream and simmer for 5 additional minutes.

Remove the pot from the heat and using a stick immersion blender, blend in the remaining cubes of butter until the sauce is completely smooth.

Suya Kebabs

These are the beef skewers your backyard barbecue dreams are made of. They're easy, too, just so long as you get everything marinating ahead of time. Beef suya is the Nigerian take on shish kebabs, skewered and grilled and served with additional sides of peanuts and lime juice. Normally, it's super spicy.

This is a significantly less fiery suya mix, which you can adjust to your spice sensibilities. Marinate thinly sliced beef, then grill it on skewers. I like this served alongside grilled plantain, which is a delicious way to slow down the beef intake. You can also do suya with shrimp or chicken. For a sweeter take on the dish, try the suya with Bourbon Apricot Dried Fruit Compote (page 216). You can tell your friends, "You barbecue and I'll suya."

4 to 6 servings

PREP TIME
*3 hours
15 minutes
(including
marinade time)*
COOKING TIME
6 to 10 minutes
TOTAL TIME
*3 hours
25 minutes*

2 bird's-eye chiles,
  seeded and chopped
1 tablespoon onion powder
1 tablespoon garlic powder
1 teaspoon smoked paprika
juice and finely grated zest of 4 limes

1 cup vegetable oil
1 pound flank or sirloin steak,
  sliced against the grain into
  ¼-inch-thick strips
1 teaspoon kosher salt

Whisk together the chiles, onion powder, garlic powder, paprika, lime juice and zest, and oil in a medium bowl until completely combined.

Using your hands, coat the beef in the marinade, making sure each piece is thoroughly covered. Place in a nonreactive container, cover, and put in the refrigerator to marinate for around 3 hours.

Soak bamboo skewers in water to cover for 1 hour.

Remove the meat from the marinade and thread the beef strips onto each skewer accordion style, making sure the meat is not bunched up.

Prepare a charcoal grill or preheat a cast-iron grill pan over high heat.

Season the meat with the salt. Place on the hot grill and cook for about 3 minutes on each side, turning with tongs once browned and caramelized.

Suya Kebabs

Grilled Wagyu Burger *with* Gruyère *and* Vidalia Onion Spread

Who doesn't love burgers? The fun of making them is finding your own special spin. Alexander's favorite cheese is Gruyère, so we started with that.

Tomatoes aren't always in season. So if you're not happy with the selection at your local market, roast them for 20 minutes in the oven with olive oil, salt, and pepper. They'll caramelize a little, which will make them perfect for layering on your burger.

This burger reaches a whole new level of excellence when topped with the tangy and crunchy Pickled Cabbage Slaw (page 194).

4 servings

PREP TIME
5 minutes

COOKING TIME
10 minutes

TOTAL TIME
15 minutes

1½ pounds coarsely minced wagyu beef chuck
1 teaspoon kosher salt
½ teaspoon freshly ground black pepper
olive oil
4 slices Gruyère or cheddar cheese

4 brioche burger buns, toasted (or soft potato rolls)
4 Bibb lettuce leaves
2 ripe plum tomatoes, sliced
½ cup Vidalia Onion Spread (page 80)

Season the meat with the salt and pepper and mix well with your hands. Divide the meat evenly into four portions and form into patties.

Prepare a charcoal grill or preheat a cast-iron grill pan over medium-high heat. Brush the grill with oil. When the oil begins to smoke, add the patties.

Cook the burgers until golden brown and slightly charred on the first side, about 3 minutes. Flip the burgers and cook until golden brown and slightly charred on the second side, 3 minutes for medium-rare.

Top the burgers with the cheese slices and cover with tented foil to just melt the cheese, about 1 minute.

Place each burger on the bottom bun and top with lettuce and tomato. Spread a spoonful of the Vidalia Onion Spread on the top bun and place on top of the burger.

Makes ¾ cup

PREP TIME
10 minutes
COOKING TIME
25 minutes
TOTAL TIME
35 minutes

VIDALIA ONION SPREAD

1 tablespoon unsalted butter

1 large Vidalia onion, halved and thinly sliced

kosher salt

1 tablespoon sugar

1 tablespoon apple cider vinegar

½ bird's-eye chile, seeded and minced

3 tablespoons mayonnaise

Heat the butter in a large sauté pan over medium heat. Add the onion when the butter begins to bubble and foam. Season with a pinch of salt and cook, stirring often, until beginning to caramelize, about 15 minutes. Stir in the sugar and vinegar.

Lower the heat and continue cooking until the onions are a deep golden brown, about 10 minutes longer.

Once caramelized, add the chile and remove from the heat.

Let the mixture cool, then transfer to a food processor. Pulse until the onion is coarsely chopped. Add the mayonnaise and pulse in quick bursts to incorporate without pureeing.

Store in an airtight nonreactive container in the refrigerator.

Yard Dog

Alexander loves hot dogs, so our challenge was to make one that fit into a fine-dining atmosphere. We chose good-quality chicken hot dogs for both flavor and health and then we topped them with our chicken chili. We also brush the hot dog buns with butter before lightly toasting them.

8 good-quality chicken hot dogs
8 New England–style hot dog buns
2 tablespoons unsalted butter, melted

2 cups Bebop Chicken Chili (page 71)
1 cup shredded cheddar cheese
2 scallions, chopped

Bring 1 inch of water to a simmer in a large skillet. Add the chicken dogs and cook to plump and heat through, 5 to 8 minutes.

Heat a large cast-iron griddle pan over medium heat. Brush sides of hot dog buns with the melted butter and griddle them, turning, until deeply golden brown, about 30 seconds per side.

Add the hot dogs to the griddle pan, turning often to crisp the casings, about 2 minutes. Place the crispy-skinned dogs in the buns and top each with ¼ cup chili.

Garnish with the cheese and scallions.

8 servings

PREP TIME
5 minutes
COOKING TIME
10 minutes
TOTAL TIME
15 minutes

Oxtails

There's a comfort to cooking with oxtails. It's a dreamy piece of meat: It has the rich texture and flavor components that every chef dreams of—the fattiness of some cuts near the base, the leanness of others closer to the tip, and the bone marrow. It's like picking up a spare rib.

Oxtail is kind of like the beef version of collards: frequently looked down on and misunderstood, and often cooked within an inch of its life. It's also one of the more affordable cuts of beef available. In Asian (especially Korean), African, or Caribbean cuisine, oxtails are most often used in stews and soups and served with a starch like rice.

The oxtail braising liquid is like a pot of gold that you can keep in your fridge, and it will add rich depth to everything you make. You can use it to flavor beans and soups or to add a layer of complexity to our chili recipe (page 71) or to stewed meat like short ribs. Use it anywhere you might use beef stock.

Braised Oxtails

4 to 6 servings

PREP TIME
35 minutes

COOKING TIME
approximately
4 hours

TOTAL TIME
4 hours
35 minutes

¼ cup plus 3 tablespoons olive oil

4 pounds oxtail, prepped from the butcher

kosher salt

freshly ground black pepper

2 cups red wine

1 quart veal or beef stock

3 cinnamon sticks

3 bay leaves

3 oranges, quartered

1 bunch thyme

1 bunch parsley

1 jalapeño, chopped with seeds

Preheat your oven to 325°F.

Heat a large Dutch oven over medium-high heat and add 3 tablespoons of olive oil. Once the oil begins to shimmer add the oxtail in a single layer and season with salt and pepper. Sear the meat until lightly browned on all sides, turning with long tongs, about 2 minutes per side. Remove pieces to a plate as they brown.

Deglaze the pot with the red wine, making sure to bring up the brown bits of fond from the bottom of the pan with a wooden spoon. Bring wine to a full boil, then lower the heat to medium and add in the veal stock, 3 cups of water, cinnamon sticks, bay leaves, oranges, thyme, parsley, and jalapeño. Season generously with pepper.

Cover and braise in the oven for 3 to 4 hours until the meat is tender and falling off the bone. Check periodically to make sure there's a sufficient liquid level and stir the braise to make sure the bottom doesn't stick. Let the meat cool and then remove it from the liquid and shred by hand. Strain the braising liquid, discarding solids in the strainer.

If you're unsure of what wine to cook with when following recipes, a good rule of thumb is to use a wine that has a moderate alcohol content (ideally between 10 to 13 percent) and that would normally pair well with the main ingredient of the dish. For example, a dry red wine such as merlot for braised red meat dishes.

Don't throw out the braising liquid! After removing the oxtail, refrigerate or freeze the flavor-packed liquid for future use in a soup, sauce, or stew.

CHEF JJ'S KITCHEN TIPS

Tamarind Glazed Oxtails

Tamarind is this tangy, West African fruit that can be a great building block for a barbecue-like sauce. Jarritos makes a tangy/sweet tamarind soda, and my great aunt soaked tamarinds in rum along with other fruits when she made her holiday fruit cakes every year. The island flavors of this dish never fail to transport me to the warm weather and good food of a West Indian Day parade.

½ cup tamarind paste

1 cup ketchup

1 tablespoon Dijon mustard

¼ cup apple cider vinegar

¼ teaspoon ground five-spice powder

¼ cup dark brown sugar

3 cups pulled meat from Braised Oxtails (page 84)

Brown Rice Grits (page 177)

Pickled Cabbage Slaw (page 194)

Combine the tamarind, ketchup, mustard, vinegar, five-spice powder, and brown sugar in a small pot over medium heat. Simmer the sauce for about 10 minutes, stirring often until it thickens slightly. Pour through a fine strainer and let cool.

Preheat the broiler to medium.

Place the braised oxtail on a foil-lined baking sheet and coat with the tamarind glaze. Broil for 5 to 10 minutes, until the glaze is slightly caramelized.

Plate the oxtail over the grits and top with slaw.

8 servings

PREP TIME

35 minutes

COOKING TIME

1 hour

(including

cooling time)

TOTAL TIME

1 hour

35 minutes

Oxtail Dumplings *with* Green Apple Curry

6 to 8 servings

PREP TIME
45 minutes

COOKING TIME
*20 minutes
(including
cooling time)*

TOTAL TIME
*5 hours
45 minutes*

There are three parts to this dish, which is why it's easy to be scared off. You have your oxtail filling to contend with, then the dumpling wrappers, and the green apple curry sauce. You can always buy dumpling wrappers to save time (in fact, I urge you to do this), but the rest is really about dividing your efforts, or cooking with someone else and working in parallel. The dumplings can even stand on their own with a simpler sauce, but the green apple curry adds an unexpected brightness to it all as opposed to the rote saltiness that you may get with a soy-based sauce. Not to mention that fruit curry brings the flavors of the Caribbean to life.

1 tablespoon olive oil
½ cup minced shallots
2 tablespoons minced fresh ginger
3 scallions, thinly sliced
1 Thai chile, minced
1 cup shredded Savoy cabbage
½ teaspoon ground turmeric
½ teaspoon curry powder

1 cup shredded Braised Oxtail meat (page 84)
1 (12-ounce) package thin wonton wrappers (48 wrappers)
kosher salt
egg wash, as needed
Green Apple Curry Sauce (page 91)
fresh cilantro

In a medium sauté pan, heat the oil over medium-high heat. Lightly sweat the shallots and ginger in the oil for about 3 minutes, stirring with a flexible spatula.

Add the scallions, chile, and cabbage and sauté. Once the cabbage has become soft and translucent, about 5 minutes, stir in the turmeric and curry powder. Remove from the heat and let cool.

Add the shredded oxtail meat and the cabbage mixture to a food processor. Gently pulse to chop and combine the ingredients.

To assemble the dumplings: lay out wonton wrappers in a single layer on damp towels. Add 1 teaspoon of the cabbage mixture to the center of each wrapper. Wet the edges of the wonton with egg wash using your finger. Fold the filled wrapper in half to form a triangle, then bring the bottom corners together to finish the fold. Use a bit more egg wash for the bottom corners.

Boil the wontons in salted water for 3 to 4 minutes. Make sure to boil them in batches and not overcrowd the pot.

Serve the dumplings over the curry sauce, garnished with cilantro.

When assembling wontons, make sure to press as much air out of the wontons as you can while sealing them to keep them from falling apart while boiling.

As you're making dumplings, the best way to ensure they don't stick together is to store them in a container with at least two inches of cornmeal.

GREEN APPLE CURRY

- 1 tablespoon curry powder
- 2 cloves garlic, chopped
- ½ cup chopped shallots
- 1 tablespoon ginger, minced
- 1 jalapeño, chopped
- ½ stalk lemongrass, bruised and chopped
- 4 green apples, peeled, cored, and chopped
- 1¼ cup canned coconut milk
- ¼ cup fresh lime juice
- kosher salt and freshly ground black pepper, to taste
- ½ pound (2 sticks) unsalted butter, cubed

In a dry sauté pan over medium heat, toast, while constantly stirring, the curry powder with the garlic, shallots, ginger, jalapeño, and lemongrass for about 2 minutes, until the aroma of the spices and aromatics begin to come out.

Add the apples and 2 tablespoons of water and cook over a medium-low heat, stirring with a flexible spatula. Stir in the coconut milk and simmer for 20 minutes, stirring frequently. Add in lime juice and season with salt and pepper.

Before removing the sauce from the low flame slowly add in the cubed butter. Whisk in one cube at a time, only adding the next once incorporated, making the sauce rich and creamy.

Makes 4 cups

PREP TIME
15 minutes
COOKING TIME
20 minutes
TOTAL TIME
35 minutes

If you prefer a completely smooth curry, strain the sauce before adding in the lime juice and butter.

BBQ Brisket Egg Roll

This is a great dish to make the Sunday after you've had brisket. You can buy the egg roll wrappers at Whole Foods or your local Asian market. If you have leftover brisket, you could have this dish on the table in less than an hour. You can also buy premade brisket at your favorite market.

6 servings

PREP TIME
30 minutes
COOKING TIME
15 minutes
TOTAL TIME
45 minutes

1 pound Smoked Brisket (page 94 or store bought), finely chopped
2 cups Gumbo Spice BBQ Sauce (page 95)
12 (6-inch square) egg roll wrappers
1 cup Sautéed Cabbage (page 95)
vegetable oil (for baking or deep-frying)

In a large bowl, combine the brisket and about ½ cup of the barbecue sauce. Make sure there is enough sauce to moisten the meat but not overly saturate it.

Lay each egg roll wrapper flat on a clean, dry work surface. Evenly fill the center of each wrapper with about 2 tablespoons of the brisket mixture and 1 tablespoon of the cabbage. Leave a ½-inch border around the edges of the wrapper.

Using your finger, moisten the top portion of the wrapper with water.

Starting at the bottom, fold the lower portion of the wrapper over the brisket filling. Tuck in each of the sides, as you would wrap a burrito. Continue rolling up from the bottom. Press to seal the moistened wrapper edge to the roll. Turn over to keep the seal at the bottom.

To bake the egg rolls: Preheat the oven to 350°F.

Heat ¼ cup of the oil in a large sauté pan. Working in batches, brown the egg rolls, turning to cook them evenly in the hot oil, about 2 minutes per batch. Transfer them to a wire rack set over a baking sheet. Once all the egg rolls are browned, transfer the rack and baking sheet to the oven and bake for about 10 minutes, until heated through.

To deep-fry the egg rolls: Fill a large Dutch oven halfway with oil and heat it to 350°F. Working in batches of four, and returning the oil to 350°F before each batch, fry the egg rolls until golden, turning occasionally, about 2 minutes; drain on paper towels.

Serve the egg rolls with extra BBQ sauce on the side.

Cover the egg roll wrappers with a damp paper cloth or dish cloth while they're waiting to be filled. This will keep the wrappers from drying out.

If you are deep-frying your egg rolls, it is extremely important that the wrappers are sealed well, so they do not fall apart while frying.

10 to 12 servings

SMOKED BRISKET

PREP TIME
1 hour
COOKING TIME
7 hours
TOTAL TIME
8 hours

2 tablespoons dried oregano

2 tablespoons dried thyme

1 teaspoon powdered bay leaf

2 tablespoons onion powder

2 tablespoons garlic powder

1 teaspoon ground cayenne

2 tablespoons brown sugar

2 tablespoons smoked paprika

3 tablespoons salt

1 tablespoon freshly ground black pepper

1 cup vegetable oil

1 (6- to 8-pound) whole beef brisket

Combine all ingredients but the beef in a large bowl and stir until the mixture looks almost loose and muddy in appearance.

Place the brisket on a baking sheet and pat dry. Cover the brisket completely with the rub blend, making sure to flip the brisket and cover the underside as well. Tent the seasoned meat with foil and let marinate for no longer than 1 hour at room temperature.

While the meat melds with the rub spices, prep your smoker or grill with cherry or apple wood.

Place the brisket, fatty side up, on the grill grate as far away from the heat source as possible. Cover the grill and smoke the meat, undisturbed, for 45 minutes.

Meanwhile, preheat the oven to 250°F.

Carefully remove the brisket from the grill and wrap it in foil; place it on a baking sheet and place in the oven. Cook until the meat reaches an internal temperature of 190 to 200°F, 4 to 6 hours. The brisket is finished cooking when it is very tender but not quite falling apart. Let it rest for 15 minutes, then unwrap and slice, against the grain, in ¼-inch slices.

SAUTÉED CABBAGE
Makes 4 cups

- 2 tablespoons olive oil
- 1 large onion, thinly sliced
- 1 teaspoon minced fresh ginger
- 1 bird's-eye chile, seeded and minced
- 1 head cabbage, quartered and sliced (about 2 pounds)
- kosher salt and freshly ground black pepper

Heat a large sauté pan over medium-high heat, then add the oil. When the oil is hot, add the onion and sauté to soften slightly, about 2 minutes. Stir in the ginger and chile. Cook for an additional 2 minutes.

Add the cabbage and salt and pepper to taste and stir to combine. Reduce the heat to medium and sauté for 10 to 15 minutes, stirring occasionally and adding a touch of water if the pan is too dry. Cook until the cabbage is tender and begins to caramelize. Season to taste.

GUMBO SPICE BBQ SAUCE
Makes 3 cups

- 1 tablespoon Gumbo Spice Mix (page 64), or your favorite preblended gumbo spice mix
- 1 teaspoon kosher salt
- 2 cups ketchup
- ¼ cup Dijon mustard
- ¼ cup apple cider vinegar
- 3 tablespoons Worcestershire sauce
- ½ teaspoon hot sauce
- ¾ cup dark brown sugar

Whisk together all the ingredients in a small saucepan over medium-high heat. Bring to a simmer and cook for 5 minutes. Remove from the heat and let cool before using. Cover and refrigerate for up to 1 week.

Feijoada *with* Black Beans *and* Spicy Lamb Sausage

eijoada is known as the gumbo of Brazil, but it's a dish that beautifully illustrates all the ways in which the global spice trade and the African diaspora set the table for dishes that are beloved all over the world. You'll find feijoada everywhere from Macau to Mozambique, from Angola to Cape Verde to Goa.

This recipe is layered with flavors, starting with the Spicy Black Beans (page 98) and the complex, umami taste of the oxtail braising liquid.

To add a contrasting texture in the dish, separately sear the braised oxtail in a sauté pan over high heat with a touch of olive oil. Sear for about 2 minutes on each side or until the meat achieves a nice caramelized crust. Deglaze the pan with a touch of the feijoada liquid before removing the oxtail and serving.

6 servings

PREP TIME
30 minutes

COOKING TIME
3 hours

TOTAL TIME
*3 hours
30 minutes*

1 tablespoon olive oil
1 pound spicy lamb sausage
3 cups Spicy Black Beans
   (page 98), drained
2 cups pulled braised oxtail meat,
   with 3 cups braising liquid reserved
   (page 84), plus 6 pieces whole braised
   oxtail

kosher salt and freshly ground black
   pepper
1 tablespoon fresh lime juice
Jollof Rice (page 178) or
   steamed long-grain white rice
½ cup chopped fresh cilantro
2 cups orange segments
   (from 2 oranges)

In a large Dutch oven, heat the oil over medium-high heat. When the oil begins to shimmer, add the sausage and cook until it is slightly charred and browned.

Add the black beans. Once the beans are heated through, add the pulled oxtail meat and pour in the braising liquid. Bring to a simmer and lower the heat to medium. Cook uncovered for about 30 minutes and let the liquid simmer slowly and reduce to thicken slightly and build flavor.

Season with salt and pepper to taste.

Remove from the heat and finish with lime juice just before serving.

Spoon over rice, top each dish with whole braised oxtail on the bone, garnish with the cilantro and orange segments, and serve.

Feijoada is an extremely versatile stew that can take many forms. The layered flavors from the spicy black beans and the oxtail braising liquid build the complex spice and components of this dish. It can be made with any of your favorite flavor-dense stocks in place of the oxtail liquid.

SPICY BLACK BEANS

Makes about 6 cups

1 pound dried black beans, rinsed
2 tablespoons olive oil
6 cloves garlic, minced
1 cup diced red onion
kosher salt
½ cup diced celery
½ cup diced carrots

2 bird's-eye chiles, seeded and minced
½ teaspoon ground cumin
¼ cup canned chipotles in adobo, chopped, with their sauce (about ½ [7-ounce] can)
6 cups oxtail braising liquid (page 84), beef broth, or water
freshly ground black pepper

Put the black beans in a 2-quart container and fill the container with water. Cover and refrigerate overnight. Drain the beans, discarding the water.

In a 6-quart stockpot, heat the oil over medium-high heat. When the oil begins to shimmer, add the garlic and cook for 2 minutes, until the garlic just becomes aromatic. Follow with the onion and ½ tablespoon salt to bring out the flavors and liquid from the vegetables. Cook, stirring constantly, until the onion is translucent, about 2 minutes. Add the celery, carrots, and chiles and cook for 3 additional minutes.

Stir in the cumin and cook for 1 minute, then add the chipotles and their sauce and cook to heat through. Add the soaked black beans and the oxtail braising liquid.

Lower the heat to medium and let the liquid come to a lazy simmer. Cover and let simmer and reduce for about 1 hour. Uncover the pot and use a wooden spoon to smash some of the beans against the side of the pot. Stir the smashed beans into the stew to make it extra creamy. Simmer, uncovered, for another 30 to 45 minutes, until the beans are very tender but not falling apart.

Season to taste with salt and black pepper and store, with any cooking liquid, in an airtight nonreactive container for up to 3 days.

Spiced Goat
with Sticky Rice

G oat meat is served and beloved just everywhere in the Caribbean and Africa. I don't think any other cultures have put as much thought into the best way to get the most out of this lean meat (goats run around a lot). It's not as strong as lamb, but it's both gamier and richer in taste than chicken. This is one of those simple dishes that mixes the unexpected (the goat meat) with the universally popular (sticky rice). And as you can see from this photo, it looks just as good as it tastes.

6 to 8 servings

PREP TIME
15 minutes
COOKING TIME
20 minutes
TOTAL TIME
35 minutes

2 tablespoons olive oil
2 tablespoons minced fresh ginger
3 shallots, minced
1 bird's-eye chile, seeded and finely chopped
2 pounds deboned goat shoulder or beef chuck, cut into 2-inch cubes

kosher salt and freshly ground black pepper
2 scallions, chopped
1 teaspoon ground turmeric
1 teaspoon curry powder
1 head cabbage, shredded
Coconut Sticky Rice (page 174)

Heat the oil over medium heat in a large sauté pan. Add the ginger, shallots, and chile and sauté for 3 minutes. Once the aromatics are softened, add the goat. Season with salt and pepper and cook, turning occasionally, until browned on all sides, about 10 minutes.

Stir in the scallions, turmeric, and curry powder. Make sure the meat is completely coated with the spices, then add the cabbage. Sauté until the cabbage is tender but still holds its shape, about 5 minutes.

Remove from the heat, and when the meat is cool enough to handle, chop it finely. Serve over the sticky rice.

Chicken Liver Toast *with* Asian Pear and Bird's-Eye Chile Jam

12 servings

PREP TIME
10 minutes
TOTAL TIME
10 minutes

Pâté can be blasé. But never with this recipe. Start with the best chicken liver mousse you can find, then add accompaniments that riff on the traditional flavors. There's the pome fruit—in this case pear rather than apple. The sweetness of the jam is laced with the sharp kick of bird's-eye chiles, which is instantly countered by the fat of the liver.

Chicken Liver Pâté (page 106)
12 slices white bread, toasted and cut into halves, for serving
1 medium Asian pear, sliced thinly, for serving
Bird's-Eye Chile Jam (page 219)

Spread the pâté on the toast halves and top with Asian pear slices and Bird's-Eye Chile Jam.

CHICKEN LIVER PÂTÉ

1 pound chicken livers

2 cups whole milk

1 cup Bordeaux wine

1 cup port or Madeira wine

8 tablespoons (1 stick) unsalted butter, cubed

4 cloves garlic, minced

½ cup Caramelized Onions (page 107)

1½ teaspoons kosher salt

freshly ground black pepper

½ cup heavy cream, or more if needed

Rinse the chicken livers under cold running water and place in a 2-quart container. Pour the milk over the livers, then cover and refrigerate overnight. Drain the chicken livers and pat dry.

Combine the wine in a 2-quart saucepan and cook over medium heat until it is reduced to ½ cup and has a syrupy consistency, 30 to 40 minutes. Set aside.

Preheat a large sauté pan over medium-high heat. Add 2 tablespoons of the butter to the pan and when the foaming subsides add the chicken livers. Sauté for 2 minutes.

Add the garlic, Caramelized Onions, salt, pepper to taste, and the reduced wine. Cook until the livers are firm, plump, and still slightly pink on the inside, about 2 minutes longer.

Remove the pan from the stove and put its contents in a blender or food processor. While blending the liver, slowly add the cream and the remaining cubed butter. Puree until smooth and creamy, adding a little more cream if necessary. Taste and adjust the seasoning.

CHEF JJ'S
KITCHEN
TIPS

It is important to blend the livers while still quite hot to ensure that the butter and cream get properly incorporated.

CARAMELIZED ONIONS

Makes 1 cup

- 4 tablespoons unsalted butter
- 1 pound Spanish onions, halved and sliced thinly into half moons
- ½ teaspoon kosher salt
- ½ teaspoon freshly ground black pepper
- 1 tablespoon fresh thyme

In a large cast-iron pan, melt the butter over medium-high heat. Add the onions and salt and pepper and cook, stirring constantly, until the onions begin to soften, about 5 minutes.

Stir in the thyme and cook, scraping the browned bits off the bottom of the pan frequently, until the onions are golden brown, about 20 minutes.

Make a big batch of caramelized onions all at once and refrigerate in an airtight container to use in other recipes throughout the week. Or freeze them in single servings to use for the month.

You can use extra caramelized onions on top of home fries or mix them into a fried rice or a stewed chicken dish.

CHEF JJ'S KITCHEN TIPS

Ramen *with* Crispy Duck

4 servings

PREP TIME
10 minutes

COOKING TIME
30 minutes

TOTAL TIME
40 minutes

I like this for a dinner party because much of it can be done ahead of time and it's just a matter of plating it beautifully once the noodles are good to go. Plus, there are leftovers, aka the chef's treat.

The duck breasts are seasoned with a perfect mix of Asian flavors: honey, hoisin, soy, and sesame. Then you place them in a bowl of lightly blanched ramen noodles. The flavors all come together in the broth, which is made richer by the rendered duck fat that you save from the pan you cooked it in.

2 duck breasts (about 1 pound total)
kosher salt and freshly ground black
  pepper
1 tablespoon soy sauce
1 tablespoon honey
2 cups chicken stock
1 cup sliced shiitake mushroom caps
1 teaspoon sesame oil

1 teaspoon hoisin sauce
1 teaspoon seeded and
  minced bird's-eye chile
2 shallots, sliced
1 pound ramen noodles, blanched
  (still firm and chewy)
fresh cilantro leaves
chopped scallions

Pat the duck breasts dry and score the skin with a sharp knife, cutting through to the fat but not the meat.

Heat a cast-iron pan over medium-high heat.

Season the duck with salt and pepper. When the pan is hot enough to sizzle a sprinkle of water, place the duck in the pan skin side down. Cook the breast for 5 minutes, until the skin is lightly browned, then lower the heat to medium-low. Continue cooking the skin side of the breast until the fat renders out and the skin is crisp and golden brown, 8 to 10 more minutes.

Turn the breast over and add the soy sauce and honey and cook for 3 to 5 minutes, until the meat is cooked through to just pink. Remove the pan from the heat and take the duck out of the pan.

Set the duck breast aside to rest. Remove 3 tablespoons of duck fat from the pan and save for another use. Reserve the pan with the remaining duck drippings

To make the ramen broth, place the chicken stock in a small saucepan over high heat. Bring to a boil, then reduce the heat to a simmer.

Put the duck pan back over medium heat. Add the mushrooms and sauté for 3 minutes in the rendered fat and duck juices. Add the simmering broth, the sesame oil, hoisin, chile, and shallots and simmer for 5 minutes, seasoning to taste. Remove from the heat and add the blanched ramen noodles.

Slice the duck breasts on a bias into diagonal pieces. Pour the noodles and broth into a large bowl and top with the crispy duck.

Garnish with cilantro and scallions.

High Harlem AND THE Bamboo Inn

ESSAY ⤷

U p until 1910, more than 90 percent of African Americans lived in the American South. Then came the great migration, and millions of African Americans made their way north. In the 1920s, in Harlem, an explosion of art, music, and literature arose from a generation of young artists who were coming to see the experience of blackness in a new way. "The New Negro Movement," as it was called by Alain Locke, captured the attention of the world and its effect was felt everywhere, from Josephine Baker, draped in Patou gowns, on the Paris stage, to the national popularity of Harlem stride master Duke Ellington to the popularity of Zora Neale Hurston and Langston Hughes. Infused throughout the music and art, literature and fashion, was the spark and energy of freedom. It was a universal energy that charmed and enchanted people of all colors.

So if freedom was the flame of the Harlem Renaissance, what did all of that newfound liberty taste like? There was a playfulness to how Harlemites liked to dine—and a taste for the exotic. A'Lelia Walker was an early New York It Girl. She was the only child of Madam C. J. Walker, the first self-made woman millionaire in America and a devoted patron of the arts. She called her home "the Dark Tower" in honor of noted writer Countee Cullen. A'Lelia took an insouciant tone toward cultural norms. Langston Hughes called her "the joy goddess of Harlem," and she never disappointed on that count. On one famous occasion, she served her white guests pigs' feet, chitterlings, and bathtub gin while her black guests dined on caviar, pheasant, and champagne.

Chinese food held a special place in Harlem life. Wallace Thurman, a popular Harlem Renaissance writer, noted that "Negroes seem to have a penchant for Chinese food—there are innumerable Chinese restaurants all over Harlem." Although there were many affordable and inexpensive Chinese restaurants, some Chinese restaurants served haute cuisine, like Hong Ping Lo restaurant in the 1880s and the popular Harlem restaurant the Bamboo Inn.

Thurman famously wrote of the Bamboo Inn as "the place to

see 'high Harlem.'" The crowd consisted of "well-dressed men escorting expensively garbed women and girls; models from *Vanity Fair* with brown, yellow and black skins. Doctors and lawyers, Babbitts and their ladies with fine manners (not necessarily learned through Emily Post), fine clothes and fine houses to return to when the night's fun has ended." Even the Savoy Ballroom, another popular jazz club in Harlem, hosted a Chinese Mandarin Ball.

The *New York Amsterdam News* in 1926 reported that an authentic "oriental" experience would take place on July 23, 1926. A Chinese kitchen would be installed and the attendees would enjoy food prepared by "a genuine oriental at prices that are lower than any place in town, but with the same high grade service and ingredients used as heretofore." History reminds us that Harlem entertained fine dining experiences and culinary tasting menus that celebrated both local and international cuisines.

At the crux of it, Harlem was—and continues to be—a community that embraces the complicated conversation of race, so politics is always on the menu. Roi Ottley noted in his 1936 article "Hectic Harlem" that "the Chinese are daily in our midst, with their restaurants and their laundries." Touching on the political, Ottley noted that during the March 1935 race riots in Harlem (incited by a police brutality case of a teenage boy), more than one Chinese restaurateur protested alongside African Americans, declaring, "Me colored too."

In the early twentieth century, when Chinese restaurants moved uptown, the menus were continuously overhauled to reflect both the Southern taste palate (since that is where many Harlem residents had come from) and the desire for affordable, fast, and tasty food. The *New York Tribune* noted that popular dishes in Harlem included "Yockaman," "chop suey," and "chow man." Ottley wrote that in Harlem, African Americans "only order pork fry rice and chicken chop suey . . . and ignore the more delicate and native Chinese dishes." Although the option of the Chinese fine dining experience was present in Harlem, Chinese restaurants quickly became known as an inexpensive option. According to Yong Chen, author of *Chop Suey USA: The Story of Chinese Food in America*, "It is the less privileged, such as marginalized whites, northern urban African Americans, and European Jews, who embraced Chinese food and formed a critical initial customer base. They chose the Chinese food represented by inexpensive dishes—a choice that shaped the entire nature of the American Chinese cuisine."

Chinese food began to infiltrate popular hip-hop culture in a big way throughout the 1980s and '90s. You can see it in the writings of Eddie Huang, author of the critically acclaimed book *Fresh Off the Boat*. The Chinese restaurant referenced in songs and film has been referred to, affectionately, as "hood Chinese." These restaurants served both classic American-style dishes as well as fried chicken wing combos and other staples of soul food cooking. In return, they were name-checked in hip-hop songs from the Fugees to A$AP Ferg.

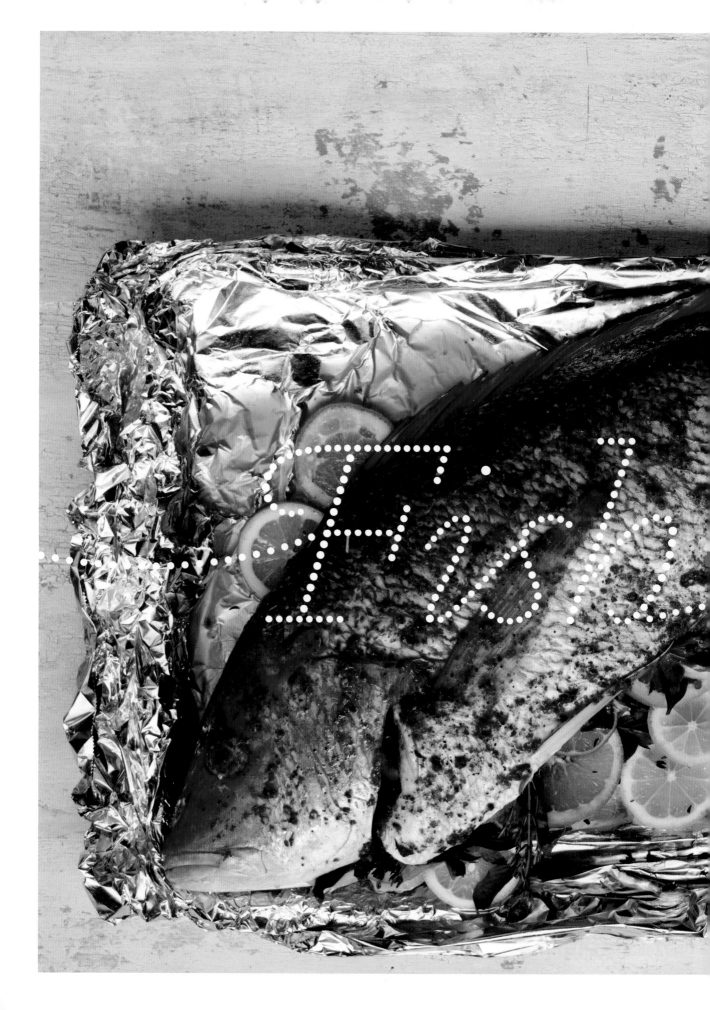

Roasted Market Fish: Whole Snapper

6 to 8 servings

PREP TIME
30 minutes

COOKING TIME
30 minutes

TOTAL TIME
60 minutes

Most people don't think of West Africa as a beach destination. But, of course, it sits right on the Atlantic. This recipe was inspired by my time in Ghana and the weekends on Labadi Pleasure Beach. Grilling on the beach is a Sunday tradition. When I'm back home in Harlem, I think that roasting a whole snapper is a perfect way to channel that casual ease and elegance of cooking on the beach. And in the wintertime, nothing beats roasting for warming your home—literally and figuratively.

1 (6-pound) whole red snapper, scaled and cleaned, with head and tail intact

juice and finely grated zest of 4 lemons
2 tablespoons red chile flakes
4 cups vegetable oil
½ teaspoon kosher salt
½ teaspoon freshly ground black pepper

Place the fish on a clean, dry surface. Use a sharp knife to score the skin of the snapper in a diamond pattern using very shallow diagonal cuts.

In a nonreactive container, combine the remaining ingredients thoroughly. Place the fish in the marinade, cover, and refrigerate for 20 minutes, turning the fish halfway through.

Preheat the oven to 450°F and place a large cast-iron pan in the oven to preheat as well.

Remove the fish from the marinade and pat dry. Discard the marinade.

Carefully remove the cast-iron pan from the oven and place the fish inside. It should sizzle upon contact. Cover the fish loosely with foil and roast for 13 to 15 minutes. Remove the foil and roast for an additional 15 minutes, until the fish is cooked through and the head of the fish easily moves when gently pushed.

Carefully transfer the fish to a serving platter with a large spatula and serve.

Salt-Crusted Salmon *with* Collard Green Salsa Verde

There are few things as impressive as a roasted side of fish. This is one of those show-off dishes that seems like it would be hard to make, but it's not. It's worth it to track down smoked salt for that extra layer of flavor. The aromatics that go in the cavity of the fish are what we call our Afro-Asian-American foundation: cilantro, bird's-eye chile, ginger, and lemongrass stalks. Thirty minutes in the oven while you whip up the bright, rich collard green salsa verde, and you're done. There's not a single dish in this cookbook that is as impressive and as easy.

6 to 8 servings

PREP TIME
10 minutes
COOKING TIME
30 minutes
TOTAL TIME
40 minutes

6 cups coarse salt (kosher salt or smoked sea salt)

6 egg whites

4 lemongrass stalks, tough outer layers removed, halved lengthwise

1 (1-inch) piece fresh ginger, sliced

1 bird's-eye chile, seeded and chopped

½ bunch fresh cilantro sprigs

1 (2-pound) side of wild salmon, skin-on, pin bones removed

2 cups Collard Green Salsa Verde (page 215)

Preheat the oven to 450°F.

Mix the salt and egg whites in a medium bowl with your hands and incorporate until the mixture feels like wet sand.

Spread 1½ cups of the salt mixture into a thin layer, in the shape of the salmon, on a baking sheet. (You may need to spread the mixture diagonally on the baking sheet.)

Arrange the lemongrass, ginger, chile, and cilantro over the bed of salt. Place the fish, skin side up, on the bed of salt and aromatics and pack the remaining salt mixture over and around the fish, molding it to the shape of the fillet, sealing the fish and aromatics inside.

Place the baking sheet in the oven and bake for 25 to 30 minutes. The salt crust should have a warm golden color almost like sand and be rock hard. Remove from the oven and let rest for 10 minutes.

Present the fish at the table within its salt crust, then, using a wooden spoon, strike the crust to crack it. Carefully lift pieces of the salt crust from the fish in large chunks. Peel back the skin, exposing the juicy, perfectly cooked fish. Divide the fish among plates. Discard the salt and aromatics.

Serve with the salsa verde.

CHEF JJ'S KITCHEN TIPS

The salt crust seals in the juices, making for an incredibly moist and flavorful fish.

You can substitute any fish of similar flesh type, such as striped bass or snapper, for the salmon.

Gullah Shrimp Mini Burgers

These two-bite wonders hail directly from Alexander's history in South Carolina and Gullah cuisine. The Lowcountry Gullah islands offer a legacy of Africa and the Caribbean on the doorstep of the American South, and their culinary and social richness can't be captured in any one thing. Which is why instead of trying that, we take inspiration from their cuisine and fly off to Asia.

6 servings

PREP TIME
10 minutes
COOKING TIME
8 minutes
TOTAL TIME
18 minutes

1 pound shrimp, peeled and deveined
1 celery stalk, chopped
1 medium egg
1 bird's-eye chile, seeded and chopped
1½ tablespoons soy sauce
½ teaspoon kosher salt
½ teaspoon freshly ground
  black pepper
2 tablespoons panko bread crumbs,

plus 2 cups for dredging
1 teaspoon finely grated lemon zest
  (from about 1 lemon)
¼ cup chopped fresh parsley
¼ cup chopped scallions
vegetable oil, for shallow frying
12 potato slider buns
Pickled Cabbage Slaw, for serving
  (page 194)

Place ¾ pound of the shrimp in a food processor. Add the celery, egg, chile, soy sauce, salt, and pepper and pulse until there is a mix of finely minced and coarsely chopped pieces of shrimp, about five 5-second pulses.

Fold the 2 tablespoons panko and the lemon zest, parsley, and scallions into the shrimp mixture to combine. Chop the remaining ¼ pound shrimp into ½-inch pieces and fold into the mixture.

Shape the mixture into twelve 1½-ounce balls. Roll the balls in panko and gently flatten into ½-inch-thick patties.

Heat ¼ inch of oil in a medium nonstick skillet over medium-high heat until the oil begins to shimmer. Place 3 shrimp patties in the pan. Reduce the heat to medium and cook until the edges turn pink and the burger looks golden, 3 to 4 minutes. Turn over and cook for 3 minutes, or until cooked through. Repeat with more oil and the remaining shrimp balls.

Place the burgers on the buns, top with the slaw, and serve.

Gullah Shrimp Mini Burgers

Moqueca
Brazilian Fish Stew

Brazil has its own take on gumbo. It's called moqueca: a savory fish stew served over rice. You can begin with our recipe, but what I've outlined here is just a template. Make this recipe your own by adding the things you love. We suggest salt cod and salmon, but if you love prawns, then throw those in. This recipe calls for yucca, but it will taste just as good with diced sweet potatoes. The secret to the bold flavor profile is the broth: green curry, tomato sauce, fish paste, coconut milk, chicken stock. Where you take things from there is up to you.

8 servings

PREP TIME
35 minutes

COOKING TIME
1 hour

TOTAL TIME
1 hour
35 minutes

1 cup baby spinach
2 tablespoons olive oil
2 cups diced carrots
½ cup diced onion
½ cup diced celery
½ cup diced yucca
¼ cup chopped garlic
1 poblano pepper, diced
1 jalapeño, seeded and diced
1 red Thai chile, seeded and diced
1 cup sliced okra
kosher salt

½ cup green curry paste
2 tablespoons tomato paste
1 tablespoon fish sauce
1 (15-ounce) can unsweetened coconut milk
4 cups chicken stock
freshly ground black pepper
½ cup chopped smoked salmon
8 ounces cod, cut into 1-inch pieces
8 large prawns
4 cups steamed rice

In a blender, puree the spinach with 2 tablespoons water until smooth. Transfer to an airtight container and chill until ready to use.

In an 8-quart pot, heat 1 tablespoon of the oil over medium heat and sauté all the chopped vegetables until lightly browned, 8 to 10 minutes. Add a pinch of salt halfway through sautéing.

Whisk in the curry paste and tomato paste and cook over low heat for 3 to 5 minutes. Make sure to continually whisk the sauce to keep it from sticking to the bottom of the pot.

Once the sauce becomes fragrant, slowly whisk in the fish sauce, coconut milk, and stock. Simmer over medium heat and occasionally stir until the broth begins to thicken and reduce, 30 to 45 minutes.

Taste and season with salt and pepper as needed.

Just before serving, add the spinach puree, smoked salmon, cod, and prawns. Gently simmer until the fish is cooked through, 5 to 8 minutes. Make sure to leave the fish in as large of pieces as possible by not overstirring.

Serve over rice.

Spicy Prawns *in* Piri Piri Sauce

6 servings

PREP TIME
2 hours
20 minutes
COOKING TIME
35 minutes
TOTAL TIME
3 hours

For me, piri piri sauce was love at first sweat. I'd gone to Ghana to teach a kitchen full of talented young chefs how to make a traditional Thanksgiving dinner. They hazed me, initiating me into their cooking by whipping up a batch of piri piri prawns, a beloved local dish. From the first bite, I literally started to sweat—it was so spicy. The whole kitchen erupted in laughter. But I fell in love with the flavors, and I knew that my less spicy version would be a restaurant standard. You can use this tomatoey, citrusy sauce with everything: over fish and meats, or tossed into a simple bowl of ramen or buckwheat noodles. It's a good back-pocket sauce, and the nice thing about making it at home is that you control the heat.

Sweat optional.

1½ pounds large prawns (about 18), peeled and deveined
juice and finely grated zest of 1 lemon (2 tablespoons juice, 1 teaspoon zest)
1 teaspoon red chile flakes

½ cup vegetable oil
2 tablespoons extra-virgin olive oil
½ cup Piri Piri Sauce (page 220)
Yam Flapjacks (page 196)

In a nonreactive container, combine the prawns, lemon juice and zest, chile flakes, and vegetable oil. Place in the refrigerator to marinate for 1 to 2 hours.

Remove the prawns from the marinade and pat dry with a paper towel; discard the marinade. Place a large sauté pan over medium heat and add the olive oil. Once the oil begins to shimmer, carefully add the prawns in a single layer. Cook over medium-high heat for 1 minute on each side, or until just seared.

Add the piri piri sauce to the skillet and stir to coat evenly. Bring to a simmer and cook until the prawns are cooked through and glazed with the sauce, about 3 minutes.

Remove from the heat and serve with the flapjacks.

CHEF JJ'S KITCHEN TIPS

Don't forget to properly clean the prawns before cooking by making a shallow slit in the back of each with a small knife and removing the black vein with your fingers.

Citrus Jerk Bass *with* Fonio

Jerk dishes take me back, way back. First to my great-aunt, whose cooking connects me to the West Indies every time I get a taste of pork or chicken that's been dry rubbed with that island mix. The irony is that as a kid, growing up in a family that hailed from Barbados and Puerto Rico, I didn't really like island food. I wanted to eat American food like meat loaf and spaghetti. But once I became a chef, I fell in love with all the flavors I grew up with. This is basically my homage to my aunt's recipe. All I've done here is add citrus to it to brighten up the flavors. The notes of orange, lemon, and lime in this dish make it a perfect pairing with our Oleo Saccharum Demerara syrup (page 227). This syrup is the base for any citrus cocktail.

4 to 6 servings

PREP TIME
*2 hours
20 minutes*
COOKING TIME
10 minutes
TOTAL TIME
*2 hours
30 minutes*

¼ cup soy sauce
1 tablespoon Worcestershire sauce
1 teaspoon chopped fresh thyme
1 scallion, chopped
1 clove garlic, whole
¼ Scotch bonnet pepper, chopped with seeds, or more to taste
1 teaspoon chopped fresh ginger
½ teaspoon ground allspice
1 teaspoon whole black peppercorns

2 tablespoons orange juice
1 tablespoon fresh lemon juice
1 teaspoon finely grated lemon zest
1 tablespoon finely grated lime zest
½ teaspoon kosher salt
1 teaspoon brown sugar
2 tablespoons vegetable oil
6 (4-ounce) bass fillets, skin on and descaled
Fonio (page 128)

Combine all the ingredients except the fish and fonio in a blender and puree until smooth and completely combined.

Take the fish and lightly score the skin diagonally in four places with a sharp knife, making sure not to cut too deeply. Place the fish in a nonreactive container with a lid and cover with the jerk marinade. Cover and refrigerate for at least 2 hours and up to 12 hours.

Preheat the oven to 350°F and put a cast-iron grill pan in the oven to heat until it's very hot (test by sprinkling a drop of water on the pan to see if it sizzles).

Remove the fish from the marinade and pat dry. Place in the hot pan skin side down and cook for 5 to 6 minutes. Turn the fish over and cook for 5 more minutes, until the fish flakes easily with a fork. Remove from the pan and serve over fonio.

Makes 3 cups,
4 to 6 servings

FONIO

2 tablespoons olive oil
1 teaspoon minced ginger
1 teaspoon minced garlic
¼ cup small-diced shallots
½ cup sliced okra
½ cup grape tomatoes
1 cup fonio, rinsed
¼ cup torn Thai basil

In a 2-quart saucepan, heat the oil over medium heat. Sweat the ginger, garlic, and shallots and cook for 3 minutes, until the onion becomes translucent. Add the okra and tomatoes.

When the tomatoes burst, add the fonio and stir with the vege-tables to coat. Add 1½ cups of water, bring to a simmer, cover tightly with the lid, and turn the heat to low. Cook for about 20 minutes.

Fluff with a fork and let it steam for 5 minutes. Stir in the torn Thai basil.

. . . .

Curry-Crusted Cod
with Hominy Stew

6 servings

PREP TIME
15 minutes
COOKING TIME
45 minutes
TOTAL TIME
1 hour

The secret to this dish is the cornmeal in the crust. You've got beautiful white cod, and the Indian curry gives it an aromatic golden color and flavor, but the cornmeal gives the crust this perfect texture. The hominy stew is just a bridge back to the cornmeal crust.

We love cooking with hominy because it's one of those migra-tion dishes that's such a connector. You see it in West Africa, you see it in the American South and in Puerto Rico, then you see it

in Mexico as posole. It's global comfort food that gets elevated by the elegance of the curry-crusted fish.

8 ounces bacon, diced

2 Spanish onions, diced

kosher salt

3 tablespoons minced garlic

1 jalapeño, seeded and diced

3 poblano peppers, diced

2 (15-ounce) cans white hominy corn, rinsed and drained

1 (15-ounce) can stewed tomatoes

4 cups chicken stock

3 tablespoons fresh lime juice

1 teaspoon finely grated lime zest (from about ½ lime)

¼ cup chopped fresh cilantro

freshly ground black pepper

¼ cup cornmeal

¼ cup all-purpose flour

1 tablespoon curry powder

3 tablespoons olive oil

6 (1½-inch-thick) cod fillets

Heat a 6-quart pot over medium heat. Add the bacon and cook to begin rendering the fat. Once the bacon is sizzling and a bit crispy, about 5 minutes, transfer to paper towels to drain. Add the onions to the pot and sprinkle with salt. Cook until soft and translucent, about 5 minutes. Stir in the garlic and cook for 2 minutes, until the garlic becomes fragrant. Add the jalapeño and poblano peppers and stir to cook.

Once the vegetables are soft and just beginning to brown slightly, add the hominy and stir to combine and bring up any fond at the bottom of the pan. Add the tomatoes and stock. Cover the pot and lower the heat to a simmer. Simmer the stew for 25 minutes, then uncover and simmer for 10 more minutes, or until the liquid is slightly reduced and thickened. Finish the stew by stirring in the lime juice, lime zest, and cilantro. Season with salt and pepper.

While the stew is simmering, prepare the cod: In a small bowl, combine the cornmeal, flour, and curry powder. Brush the cod fillets with 1 tablespoon of the oil and season with salt and pepper on both sides. Dredge the fish in the flour mixture and thoroughly shake off any excess flour.

Heat a large cast-iron pan over medium heat. Add the remaining 2 tablespoons oil and when it shimmers, add the cod fillets and cook until the fish is opaque and flaky, 3 to 5 minutes per side.

Serve the fish over a bowl of the stew and top with the reserved bacon.

Crispy Soft-Shell Crab *with* Avocado

4 servings

PREP TIME
10 minutes

COOKING TIME
8 minutes

TOTAL TIME
18 minutes

Timing and heat are key with soft-shell crabs. Frying them quickly in very hot oil makes them crispy, crunchy, and moist. Also, make all components for the dish before frying the crab, as they're best when eaten right away.

I like to add a hibiscus glaze to our soft-shell crabs. It's simple to make, easy to apply, and gives you a pop of flavor you won't soon forget.

If you look at the photo on page 134, you'll see that the hibiscus syrup also gives the crabs this vibrant reddish orange color, making them instantly Instagram worthy—no filters necessary.

2 medium ripe avocados, coarsely chopped
2 tablespoons chopped fresh cilantro
1 tablespoon fresh lemon juice
kosher salt
vegetable oil for deep-frying
⅔ cup all-purpose flour
½ cup cornstarch

1 egg, beaten
1 cup cold soda water
4 large soft-shell crabs (purchased precleaned)
freshly ground black pepper
2 tangerines, sliced
Hibiscus Syrup (optional; page 135)

In a medium nonreactive bowl, mash together the avocados, cilantro, lemon juice, and a pinch of salt with a fork or potato masher just until the mixture is chunky. Cover tightly with plastic wrap, pressing it right against the avocado to not let any air in. Set aside.

Pour 2 inches of oil into a large Dutch oven and heat over medium-high heat to 350°F.

In a medium bowl, combine the flour, cornstarch, and a pinch of salt and then whisk in the egg. Just before frying the crab, whisk in the cold soda water. The batter should be bubbly, a little lumpy, and thin; make sure to not overmix the batter.

Pat the crabs dry and season with salt and pepper on both

sides. Dip the crabs into the batter two at a time and let the excess batter drip back into bowl. Carefully slip into the hot oil, top side down. Fry for 1½ minutes per side, turning with tongs, until golden brown and crisp. Drain on paper towels and immediately season with salt. Repeat the process with the remaining crabs.

Serve right away alongside the avocado mash and garnished with tangerine slices. This can also be topped with the glaze.

HIBISCUS SYRUP

Makes 1 cup

- 1 cup palm sugar (or dark brown sugar)
- 1 cup dried hibiscus flowers (about 1 ounce, or 12 hibiscus tea bags)
- 2 (¼-inch-thick) slices fresh ginger
- 1 bird's-eye chile, seeded

PREP TIME
5 minutes
COOKING TIME
45 minutes
TOTAL TIME
50 minutes

In a 2-quart saucepan, combine 2 cups water and the palm sugar and heat until the sugar dissolves. Add the hibiscus, ginger, and chile, reduce to a simmer, and cook until the syrup is reduced enough to coat the back of a spoon, about 45 minutes. The color from the flowers will turn the liquid a bright pink hue.

Strain the syrup through a fine-mesh strainer; discard the solids. The syrup will continue to thicken as it cools. Let cool completely before using.

This syrup is simple to make and great for adding a pop of flavor and cutting through the richness of fried dishes.

CHEF JJ'S
KITCHEN
TIPS

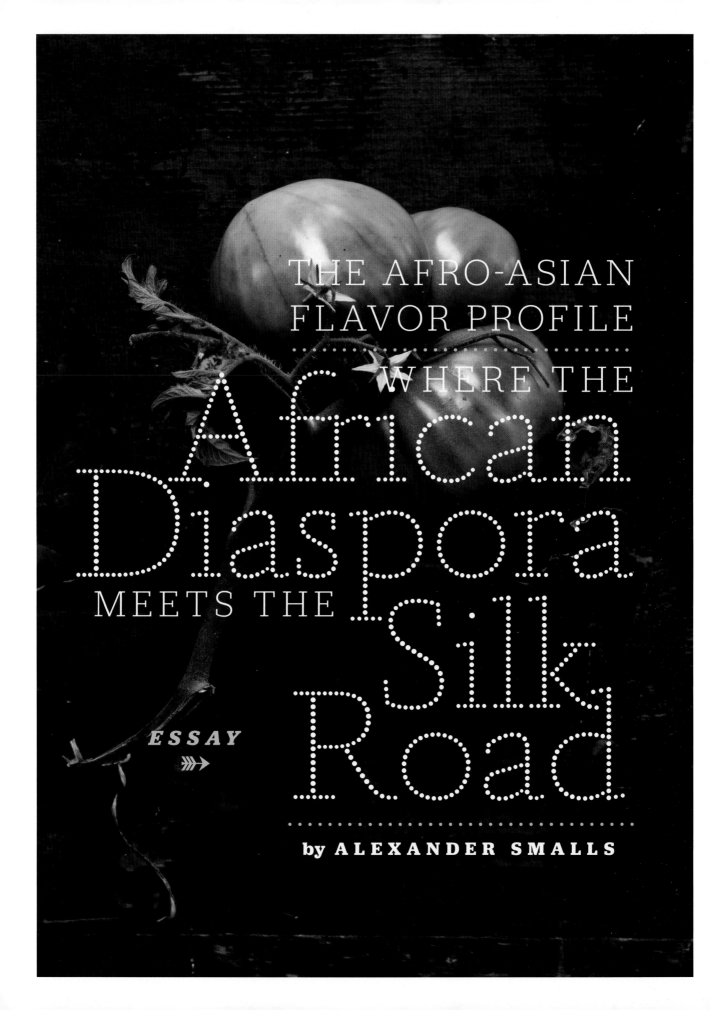

THE AFRO-ASIAN
FLAVOR PROFILE

WHERE THE
African
Diaspora
MEETS THE
Silk
Road

ESSAY ⫸

by **ALEXANDER SMALLS**

For centuries the institution of the African slave trade throughout Africa, Asia, Europe, North America, and South America helped build the agricultural and industrial revolution in an expanding world of exploration and civilization. African people labored in the fields and kitchens creating the foundation of this new world while developing a new cooking expression wherever they found themselves. They were resilient people working the land, farming, creating a legacy of food preparation and hospitality throughout the world, infusing African traditions and history in every dish along the way.

In search of the authentic roots of the African bounty, I have dedicated much of my professional curiosity, passion, and intellectual thrust, as well as my cooking skills, to educating myself and those who regard the treasure trove of this great cooking through my many restaurants, my catering event company, Smalls and Company, and dinners hosted in my New York apartment over the years. My convictions as an ambassador for the foods of the African diaspora began, in earnest, with my days as chef and restaurateur at this beloved dowtown restaurant Cafe Beulah. My years of research, travel, and scholarship hopefully merit consideration in the company of respected culinary historians. Women like Toni Tipton-Martin, the author of the book *The Jemima Code,* which the *New York Times* asked me to write about for the *Book Review.* And educator and author Jessica Harris, a friend and scholar who mirrors my commitment and enthusiasm in her many books, speeches, and activism on the subject. These ladies give me permission and strength. I'm inspired and emboldened by them, as I am by the many African-American chefs, cooks, and hospitality workers who toil in the field and on whose shoulders I stand.

Slavery? Nobody wanted to own it. The enslavers made us embarrassed that we were slaves. The enslavers didn't want to talk about it because of how it made them feel. And so because we don't like to talk about slavery in the United States, if not the world, we reduced the culinary contribution of African-heritage people to the extraordinarily flimsy rubric of "soul food," which, to my mind, represents a small fraction of our enormous contribution to global cooking. I felt, from my earliest days in the culinary community, a commitment to uncover and illuminate the story of how Africa has shaped our dining traditions and what our African and African-American ancestors truly gifted the world.

> *Slaves were the culinary game changers. There, we've said it.*

Through slavery, Africa changed the global culinary conversation. Because African slaves built, through their labor and their farming skills, the agricultural platform for every country they went to. They took their seeds, their ingredients, and their cooking techniques and changed how the world, across five continents—Africa, Asia, Europe, and North and South America—ate. But to justify slavery, slaves were categorized not as human, but as cattle, and were treated as such. In some parts of the United States, through the 1940s, African Americans were still categorized as livestock.

I wanted to allow myself to run freely under the umbrella of the diaspora. It was important for me to find the silver lining and the positivity of African cultural expression that could only come out of the ills of slavery: that was the culinary trail. It was important to me to give voice to these extraordinarily persecuted and mistreated people—my ancestors. I come from a people whose unsung contributions to the culinary world were realized through their hard work, creativity, imagination, determination, and endurance. These are the people whose harvests and culinary talents set the American table: then, now, and for years to come.

This is the food of survival and imagination, the celebration of life being a gift even when times are tough and of the promise that each new day offers. Resilient African people worked the land, farming and creating a legacy of food preparation and hospitality throughout the world while infusing African traditions and history into every dish.

The Afro-Asian-American profile first started to take root in my childhood. I grew up in Spartanburg, South Carolina, but because my family was from the Lowcountry—Charleston, Beaufort, and the Gullah islands—the food references of my life strongly came from this area, largely influenced by West Africa because it was one of the largest slave ports in the New World. West Africa influenced the cooking there, along with the French Creole and the Far East. You hear chefs talk about fusion cooking all the time. This was the original fusion: fusion as a result of migrating people.

But don't call it soul food. Don't call it soul food! That's always been a rallying cry for me. The idea that black folks who cook are only making soul food is frightening. What we have to say is much bigger than that. It's our job to expand the conversation.

The Chinese and Vietnamese migrated to western Africa in the nineteenth and early twentieth centuries. They brought rice and noodles. Now western Africa is the second largest rice-consuming region in the world, after China. We're not even talking about the whole continent of Africa. We're talking about western Africa. Jessica Harris writes in *Zester Daily*:

> *Wherever okra points its green tip, Africa has been, and the trail of trade evidenced by the presence of the pod is formidable. It turns up in the cooking of North Africa and the Middle East, where it is known as* Bamia *or* bamya. *It makes a savored curry in India, where it is called* bhindi *in Hindi. It is known as lady's fingers by those of more colonial persuasion. It's known as* jiao dou *in Chinese and* kacang bendi *in Malay. Spain takes its word for the pod from the Bantu languages of Central Africa and calls it* quingombo *or* ginbombo, *and the Brazilian variant* quiabo *seems to derive from the same origins. Our American use of the word* okra *comes from the Igbo language of Nigeria, where the plant is referred to as* okuru. *It is the French word for okra that takes us to the heart of the matter in Louisiana, because it also harks back to the Bantu languages, but simply uses the final two syllables calling the mucilaginous pod* gombo.

Speaking of gumbo, we all love gumbo. But it didn't start in New Orleans or South Carolina. It started in Senegal, and slaves brought it with them when they migrated. Culinary game changers.

Brazil enters the conversation through dishes like feijoada and moqueca. Our versions of those dishes pay tribute to the African people of Bahia in Brazil, who worked the sugar plantations that provided the economic foundation for prosperity in South America.

We talk about slavery and migration a lot because for us, it's our living history. We wouldn't have felt the importance and intensity of purpose for this food if our personal commitment to celebrating the legacy of the diaspora didn't run so deep. My restaurant teams have always mirrored our beliefs and our misson. We are a rainbow of African, African American, Latin, Tibetan, Chinese, Caribbean, and Indian . . . as well as European. The Cecil's team was the Mexican kid who's been with us from the beginning and has really come into his own. Tiffany, chef de cuisine, an amazing cook, worked with April Bloomfield at the Spotted Pig and has contributed to our success in an invaluable way. Tiffany's love for Indian food brought these flavorful techniques of Indian cooking and style uptown. Our runners were from West Africa, and they appreciated working for a restaurant that elevates Africa's culinary traditions. Our staff says it again and again: "I never thought I'd work at a restaurant where I could be proud that the foods of my heritage were served in such an elegant and celebrated way."

My vision for Afro-Asian-American cooking and the passion we've poured into this book is very simple: I want to explore the history and the culture of the foods of Africa and their intersection throughout the world . . . one plate at a time.

1 • Hibiscus	*9 • Nutmeg*
2 • Turmeric	*10 • Ginger*
3 • Cinnamon	*11 • Curry powder*
4 • Coriander seeds	*12 • Black cardamom*
5 • Sesame	*13 • Allspice*
6 • Pink peppercorns	*14 • Smoked salt*
7 • Aleppo pepper	*15 • Green cardamom*
8 • Szechuan peppercorns	*16 • Mustard seed*

King Mushrooms *with* Harissa Vinaigrette, Roasted Carrots, Carrot Curry Puree, *and* Cipollini Onions

Then secret to this dish is taking market-fresh vegetables, roasting them until they are crisp-tender, and then tossing them in a spicy vinaigrette. Clean eating has never tasted this good.

2 pounds king mushrooms,
  cleaned and left whole
  (or large oyster mushrooms)
6 cloves garlic, finely chopped
¼ cup olive oil
1 teaspoon kosher salt
¼ teaspoon freshly ground
  black pepper

¼ cup Harissa Vinaigrette
  (page 144)
Roasted Cipollini Onions (page 144)
Roasted Baby Carrots (page 146)
Carrot Curry Puree (page 160)

Preheat the oven to 400°F.

In a large bowl, toss the mushrooms, garlic, oil, salt, and pepper. Arrange in a single layer on a parchment-lined baking sheet.

Roast for 15 minutes, flip the mushrooms, and continue roasting for 10 to 15 minutes, until golden brown and tender. Toss the mushrooms with the vinaigrette while still warm. Serve with the Roasted Cipollini Onions, Roasted Baby Carrots, and Carrot Curry Puree.

6 servings

PREP TIME
30 minutes
COOKING TIME
30 minutes
TOTAL TIME
1 hour

HARISSA VINAIGRETTE

: 1½ teaspoons cumin seeds
: 1½ teaspoons coriander seeds
: 1 shallot, peeled
: ¼ cup loosely packed fresh mint leaves
: 2 teaspoons thyme leaves
: ¼ cup champagne vinegar
: 1 tablespoon harissa paste or red chile paste
: 1½ teaspoons Dijon mustard
: ½ cup olive oil

In a blender or food processor, grind the cumin and coriander seeds to a fine powder. Add the shallot, mint, thyme, vinegar, and harissa and blend until completely smooth.

Continue blending and add the mustard. Once combined, slowly pour in the oil until the mixture starts to thicken and emulsify.

ROASTED CIPOLLINI ONIONS

: 2 tablespoons olive oil
: 2 pounds whole cipollini onions, peeled and trimmed
: 1 teaspoon kosher salt
: ½ teaspoon freshly ground black pepper

Preheat the oven to 325°F.

Heat the oil in a large cast-iron skillet over medium heat. Add the onions and stir to coat. Season with the salt and pepper. Transfer to the oven and roast, stirring occasionally, until deeply caramelized and tender, about 30 minutes.

ROASTED BABY CARROTS

1 pound small colorful carrots, trimmed
½ cup olive oil
2 cloves garlic, chopped
1 tablespoon ground cumin
2 teaspoons ground coriander
1 teaspoon kosher salt

Preheat the oven to 500°F.

Put the carrots in a large bowl and toss with the oil, garlic, cumin, coriander, and salt. Arrange in a single layer on a foil- or parchment-lined baking sheet. Roast the carrots until they are tender and the spices are toasted, tossing once, 15 to 20 minutes.

Tofu Gnocchi *with* Black Garlic Crema *and* Scallions

This dish is gnocchi without the potato. Tofu has the same binding ingredient as potatoes do, so you can shape it like gnocchi. Then to give it that crispy sear, cook it in the pan like a pot sticker. Tofu is great at absorbing flavors, so I've added a mix of seasonings to this recipe. But feel free to throw in your favorite pepper and herbs.

This great vegetarian option introduces the unsung hero black garlic. A traditionally Asian ingredient, black garlic has a beautiful inky color and a sweet date-like texture. You can now find black garlic online or at markets like Whole Foods.

6 servings

PREP TIME
15 minutes
COOKING TIME
10 minutes
TOTAL TIME
25 minutes

1 (12-ounce) package extra-firm tofu
½ teaspoon finely grated lemon zest
2 tablespoons unsalted butter, melted
2 tablespoons chopped fresh parsley
2 tablespoons heavy cream
kosher salt

2 egg yolks
1 whole egg
2 cups all-purpose flour
2 tablespoons olive oil
Black Garlic Crema (page 148)
4 scallions, sliced diagonally

In a food processor, pulse the tofu to a fine consistency. Add the lemon zest, melted butter, parsley, heavy cream, ½ teaspoon salt, the egg yolks, and the whole egg and pulse until well combined. Add the flour and blend together until a ball of dough is formed.

Lay the dough out on a lightly floured cutting board and shape small portions of the dough into long ropes. With a knife dipped in flour, cut ropes into ¾-inch pieces.

Bring a large pot of lightly salted water to a boil. Drop the dough into the simmering water and cook for 3 to 5 minutes, until the gnocchi have risen to the top; drain well.

Heat a large sauté pan over high heat and add the oil. When the oil begins to shimmer, add the gnocchi in a single layer and sauté until golden brown on all sides, about 8 minutes. Don't stir too frequently; allow the tofu to lightly brown before moving in the pan.

Top with the crema and scallions and serve.

Makes 1½ cups   BLACK GARLIC CREMA

- 1 cup heavy cream
- ½ cup whole milk
- 4 cloves black garlic
- ¼ cup (½ stick) unsalted butter, cubed
- kosher salt and freshly ground black pepper

Combine the cream, milk, and black garlic in a small saucepan over medium heat. Bring to a simmer and cook until slightly reduced, about 10 minutes.

Blend the sauce with a stick immersion blender, adding butter cubes while blending until smooth. Season with salt and pepper to taste.

Plantain Kelewele

Traditionally, this dish is made with sweet plantains that are mixed into a batter, fried, and dusted with powdered sugar. But we do a savory version. An ice cream scoop will help you get that perfect shape: scoop out the mixture and fry it in hot oil.

5 ripe plantains
1 bird's-eye chile, seeded and minced
2 tablespoons chopped fresh parsley
2 tablespoons chopped fresh cilantro
1 cup rice flour
1 teaspoon kosher salt
½ teaspoon freshly ground black pepper
vegetable oil for frying
harissa paste for serving

Using a hand mixer or food processor, pulse the raw plantains to a chunky paste.

Transfer the paste to a bowl and stir in the chile, parsley, cilantro, rice flour, salt, and pepper, making sure all of the ingredients are evenly distributed and combined.

Let the batter rest for about 10 minutes to meld the flavors.

Heat 1 inch of oil in a heavy 8-quart pot over medium-high heat until hot and shimmering but not smoking, about 350°F.

Carefully fry heaping tablespoons of the batter in batches, making sure not to overcrowd the pot. Cook, turning often, until crispy around the edges and golden brown, about 5 minutes.

Using a slotted spoon, transfer the fried plantains to a baking sheet lined with paper towels.

Serve warm with red pepper spread.

6 servings

PREP TIME
10 minutes
COOKING TIME
10 minutes
TOTAL TIME
20 minutes

Black Bottom Bean Cake *with* Papaya Salsa

6 servings

PREP TIME
30 minutes

COOKING TIME
15 minutes

TOTAL TIME
45 minutes

At the turn of the century, the black bottom was a dance done by African Americans in the rural South. By the 1920s and the Jazz Age, it was so popular that it was featured in the Ziegfeld Follies. This dish, like that dance, has a similarly universal appeal.

When I go out with a bunch of friends, we like to share dishes, and you don't want just a bunch of meat on the table. But at home, it can be hard to break the habit of one big protein dish and a bunch of classic veggie sides.

This one is simple: black beans made into a cake with cumin and cilantro, onions, and our mirepoix. The papaya salsa is the highlight, and again I can't stay away from the bird's-eye chile. It reminds me of the homemade hot sauce that sat on every table of my parents' extended community of Caribbean family and friends.

1 tablespoon plus ½ cup olive oil
½ cup diced onion
kosher salt
½ cup diced poblano pepper
½ teaspoon ground cumin
¼ teaspoon ground cayenne
pinch of smoked paprika
2 tablespoons chopped fresh cilantro
¼ cup diced scallions

3 cups Spicy Black Beans (page 98; or canned black beans rinsed and drained), half pureed and half left whole
1½ cups panko bread crumbs
freshly ground black pepper
1 cup all-purpose flour
2 eggs
1 cup Papaya Salsa (page 154)
1 (10-ounce) package plantain chips

In a large sauté pan, heat 1 tablespoon of the oil over medium-high heat. Add the diced onion, sprinkle with salt, and cook until translucent around the edges, 3 to 5 minutes. Stir in the poblano pepper and sauté for 2 minutes. Stir in the cumin, cayenne, and paprika and let the spices toast for 2 additional minutes, then stir in the cilantro and scallions. Remove from the heat and place vegetables in a bowl.

Add the pureed and whole black beans and ½ cup panko to the sautéed vegetables. Fold to combine, taste, and season with salt and pepper.

Form six 3-inch patties and follow the steps for preparing the patties for frying:

• **Flour:** Put the flour in a flat dish (like a shallow bowl or pie plate) and dredge the patties until evenly coated, then shake off the excess flour.

• **Egg wash:** Crack the eggs into a medium flat dish and whisk. Dip the flour-coated patties into the egg wash and cover on all sides.

• **Breading:** Press the flour and egg–coated patties into a third tray of the panko. Shake off the excess and place on a baking sheet while prepping the rest of the patties.

Heat the remaining ½ cup oil in a large cast-iron pan over medium-high heat until shimmering, about 2 minutes.

Place patties in the pan without overcrowding and fry until golden, 2 to 3 minutes on each side.

Serve with the salsa and plantain chips.

PAPAYA SALSA

1 small ripe papaya, peeled, seeded, and cut into ¼-inch dice
2 red bell peppers, finely diced
1 teaspoon minced fresh ginger
1 red onion, finely diced
1 bird's-eye chile, minced
5 scallions, grilled until tender and slightly charred, chopped

2 tablespoons chopped cilantro
2 tablespoons chopped basil
2 tablespoons fresh lime juice
kosher salt and freshly ground black pepper to taste

Makes 4 cups

PREP TIME
15 minutes

TOTAL TIME
15 minutes

Gently mix together all of the ingredients in a medium bowl. Store in a covered nonreactive container.

Udon Noodles with Edamame
and West African Peanut Sauce

Udon Noodles *with* Edamame *and* West African Peanut Sauce

6 to 8 servings

PREP TIME
15 minutes

COOKING TIME
1 hour

TOTAL TIME
1 hour
15 minutes

In Brazil, there is an African population and a Japanese population that live really close together, and both grew up on udon. West African peanut sauce is the mother sauce: peanut butter, tomato paste, tomatoes, French mirepoix, and our special mirepoix. In the end it's like a pad thai with more frequent flyer mileage in its account.

There's nothing like eating noodles and pasta when the sauce is really right. West African peanut sauce provides the perfect creamy coating for the Japanese udon noodles.

1 tablespoon olive oil

1 cup julienned carrot

½ cup thinly sliced onion

2 cups Mother Africa Peanut Sauce (page 56), warmed

kosher salt for pasta water

1 pound udon noodles

1 cup shelled edamame, boiled in salted water for 5 minutes

½ cup cilantro leaves

½ cup Thai basil leaves

Heat the oil in a wok over medium heat. Stir fry the carrot and the onion for 1 minute. Add the peanut sauce and stir to coat.

In an 8-quart pot, bring water to a boil, salt it, and cook the noodles according to the package directions. Drain and add the noodles directly to the peanut sauce mixture, tossing to coat. Plate the noodles and top with edamame, cilantro, and Thai basil leaves.

Spiked Rosemary Macaroni and Cheese Pie *with* Caramelized Shallots

6 to 8 servings

Macaroni and cheese is such a Harlem staple that we knew we had to make ours special. Alexander has always done his with rosemary, which gives it a nice earthy flavor. We threw in caramelized shallots for sweetness and texture. Rosemary and shallots are both such simple adds, but also unexpected. We think this will be your new favorite mac.

PREP TIME

15 minutes

COOKING TIME

1 hour

TOTAL TIME

1 hour

15 minutes

2 tablespoons kosher salt

1 pound dried penne rigate pasta

1 tablespoon olive oil

8 shallots, peeled and left whole

4 cups heavy cream

4 cups shredded white cheddar cheese (about 1 cup)

4 cups shredded smoked Gouda cheese (about 1 pound)

2 tablespoons chopped fresh rosemary

2 teaspoons freshly ground black pepper

Preheat the oven to 375°F.

Bring 4 quarts water to a boil in a large pot; stir in 1 tablespoon of the salt and the pasta; cook according to the package directions for al dente pasta. Drain well.

While the pasta is cooking, in a large skillet over low heat combine the oil, the shallots, and 1 teaspoon of the salt. Cook the shallots over low heat until they begin to fall apart and caramelize, 20 to 30 minutes. Once caramelized, remove from the skillet and set aside.

Bring the cream to a simmer in a 4-quart saucepan over medium heat. Make sure the cream does not come to a boil. Stir in the cheeses. Add the rosemary and cook, whisking often, over medium-low heat, for 2 to 3 minutes, until melted and smooth. Remove from the heat. Whisk in the pepper and the remaining 2 teaspoons salt.

Stir in the cooked pasta and caramelized shallots.

Pour the mixture into a lightly greased 3-quart baking dish. Bake for 30 to 35 minutes, until golden brown and bubbly.

Remove from oven; let stand for 10 minutes before serving.

CHEF JJ'S KITCHEN TIPS

Make sure your mac and cheese has a creamy but not mushy texture by not overcooking the pasta in the first step. It should be slightly undercooked or to just al dente (with a little firmness when tested before draining). The pasta will continue to cook after the cheese sauce is added and the dish is baked.

Like most great sauces, the cheese sauce is best done over a low simmer. Don't rush it! Boiling the cream and cheese mixture will cause it to break and result in a gritty and not smooth sauce.

Roti *with* Black-Eyed Pea Hummus, Eggplant Puree, *and* Carrot Curry Puree

6 servings

PREP TIME
55 minutes (including dough resting time)
COOKING TIME
10 minutes
TOTAL TIME
1 hour 5 minutes

You'll find roti in Queens, Barbados, South Africa, and South Asia. I still remember going back to the Caribbean for a wedding and tucking into a chickpea roti with braised beef. The fact that it exists in nearly every location along the British slave trade route speaks volumes both about the frightening breadth of the industry and the resilience of the people involved who still managed to eke out innovation between the tragedies.

Everybody does their roti differently. In Barbados, it's super thin like a crêpe. Ours is a little thicker with layers, more like a classic Indian roti or what you might find in Trinidad.

As far as breads, roti is a very forgiving bread to make. You just roll it out, put it in a pan with butter or oil, and cook it until it's nice and golden on each side.

With the roti, you can serve three of our favorite dipping sauces. The sauce recipes you see here are the result of a dipping sauce battle with two of The Cecil's sous chefs, Jessica and Tiffany, who later became chef de cuisine. These three were our final winners. If you've never challenged your friends to a cookoff, you can start nice and easy by preparing the roti platter and asking your guests to bring their favorite dipping sauce. Winner gets bragging rights!

All three of these sauces are easy to cook and will keep for four or five days in the fridge. With the Black-Eyed Pea Hummus, you can get the peas from a can to save time. The Carrot Curry Puree is one of those aromatic dishes that will make your guests hungry before the plate is even in front of them. As a cook, you'll love the process of toasting the red curry in the pan, which releases an amazing scent. That toasting in the pan is a little tip that can work with any of your favorite spices.

4 cups all-purpose flour	Black-Eyed Pea Hummus
2 teaspoons baking powder	(page 161)
1 teaspoon kosher salt	Eggplant Puree (page 162)
¼ cup olive oil	Carrot Curry Puree (page 162)
2 tablespoons unsalted butter	

Combine the flour, baking powder, and salt in a mixing bowl. Gradually add the oil and 1 cup water while mixing and kneading the dough. Knead for about 5 minutes, until the dough is smooth. Set the dough aside for 45 minutes in a cool spot, covered with a damp kitchen towel.

Divide the dough into six equal-sized balls. On a lightly floured surface, flatten each slightly and roll out into 8-inch ovals with a rolling pin.

To cook the roti, place 1 teaspoon of the butter in a large cast-iron pan over medium heat until it sizzles but doesn't brown. Reduce the heat to medium and place one roti in the pan.

Cook for 1½ minutes, until the dough is bubbly and the crust is a light golden brown with a few darker brown spots appearing. Turn with a spatula and continue cooking for an additional 1 minute, or until the roti is puffy and browned in spots. Repeat the process with the remaining rotis. Serve immediately, with the hummus and eggplant and carrot purees.

BLACK-EYED PEA HUMMUS

5 cloves garlic, peeled

2 cups cooked black-eyed peas (or 1 [15-ounce] can black-eyed peas, rinsed and drained)

2 cups cooked chickpeas (or 1 [15-ounce] can chickpeas, rinsed and drained)

⅓ cup tahini (or you can substitute peanut butter)

¼ cup fresh lemon juice

½ teaspoon smoked paprika

½ teaspoon ground cayenne

kosher salt

⅓ cup olive oil

freshly ground black pepper

Puree the garlic in a food processor until finely chopped, then add the black-eyed peas. Pulse until chopped coarsely, scraping down the side of the bowl with a flexible spatula. Add the chickpeas, tahini, lemon juice, paprika, cayenne, and 1 teaspoon salt and blend the mixture while slowly adding the oil, until semismooth and thick.

Season to taste with salt and pepper.

6 servings

PREP TIME
10 minutes
TOTAL TIME
10 minutes

EGGPLANT PUREE

2 pounds large Japanese or medium
  Italian eggplants (about 2 eggplants)
kosher salt
2 tablespoons olive oil

5 pitted dates
1 teaspoon finely grated lemon zest
  (from about 1 lemon)
freshly ground black pepper

6 servings

PREP TIME
5 minutes

COOKING TIME
25 minutes

TOTAL TIME
30 minutes

Preheat the broiler to high.

Split the eggplants in half lengthwise, sprinkle with salt, and brush with the oil. Place the eggplants flesh side up on a rimmed baking sheet. Broil for 25 minutes, turning halfway through. The eggplants should have charred and blistered skin and completely soft and caramelized flesh.

Remove from the broiler and let cool slightly. Peel off skin from two of the eggplant halves, keeping the others with skin.

Roughly chop the grilled eggplant and blend in a food processor with the dates and lemon zest until completely smooth.

Season with salt and pepper to taste.

CARROT CURRY PUREE

1 pound carrots, peeled and chopped
4 cloves garlic, peeled
2 tablespoons olive oil
kosher salt and freshly ground black
  pepper
2 tablespoons tahini

3 tablespoons fresh lemon juice
½ teaspoon ground harissa or chili
  powder
2 teaspoons curry powder
1 teaspoon ground cumin

6 servings

PREP TIME
10 minutes

COOKING TIME
30 minutes

TOTAL TIME
40 minutes

Preheat the oven to 425°F.

On a baking sheet, toss the carrots and garlic cloves with the oil and a generous sprinkle of salt and pepper. Arrange in an even layer and roast until tender and starting to brown, about 30 minutes, turning to cook evenly. Remove from the oven and let cool.

Once the carrots and garlic have cooled to room temperature, put them in the bowl of a food processor with the remaining ingredients. Process until smooth. Taste and adjust the spices as necessary.

Bengali

ESSAY ⫸

Harlem

I t was a different kind of passing. The way that Indian Muslim seamen came to Harlem in the 1920s and '30s. While hundreds of thousands of African Americans came to Harlem in the first part of the twentieth century, so did immigrants from China, Jamaica, Barbados, the Bahamas, Puerto Rico, and Cuba. Throughout Central and East Harlem there was an overlapping diaspora. The brown mecca that was Harlem was more welcoming than the white world downtown. The father of comedian Alaudin Ullah migrated, as a teenager, to Harlem in the late 1930s. "On the Lower East Side, my father still felt he was being discriminated against," Ullah told NPR about his one-man show, *Dishwasher Dreams*. "You can be a blacker than black Bengali, but in Harlem, you're home." Harlem set the table for people of different colors and different faiths: These Bengali men became part of a larger Harlem community of Muslims that included African Americans, Africans, and Middle Easterners.

Food soon entered the picture and the welcome table in Harlem began to take on a different taste. Many newly arrived South Asian men started working in the service industry as line cooks and in hospitality as doormen. But by the 1930s, those who wanted to escape laboring in restaurants and hotels sought to run their own food carts or open their own restaurants. A decade later, East Harlem had a sizeable number of Indian Muslim hot dog vendors. The pushcart culture within Harlem's Indian community allowed for a social fabric to emerge, a place to catch up and exchange gossip; it was a way for Indians to inscribe themselves in the narrative of Harlem. Some pushcart vendors would eventually gain enough profit to open their own stores, selling herbs, curry powders, and spices.

The precedent for Indian cuisine in New York City had already been set by Chef J. Ranji Smile as early as 1899. According to Indian cuisine specialist Colleen Taylor Sen, "in October 1899, an intriguing figure in New York City restaurant history made his debut at Louis Sherry's eponymous new restaurant at Fifth Avenue and 44th Street. J. Ranji Smile was not only the country's first Asian-Indian chef; he was one of the earliest celebrity chefs and one whose culinary skills and escapades would be chronicled in the American press for the next 15 years." This would lead to the opening of the first Indian restaurant in New York City. According to Vivek Bald, author of *Bengali Harlem and the Lost Histories of South Asian America,* the city's first Indian restaurant, the Ceylon India Restaurant, may have opened in 1913 on 135th Street in Harlem. The Ceylon would later open in the theater district on 49th Street and become one of the important locations for Indian nationalist activities.

By the 1940s and '50s, several advertisements for Indian restaurants began to emerge in newspapers inviting readers to "Meet the 'Curry King' at India's Garden Inn," located on 122nd Street in Harlem. Often the advertisements promoted Indian cuisine alongside American fare at restaurants like the Pakistan Indian Restaurant on Lenox Avenue between 119th and 120th, opened in 1957. In 1958 the Bombay India Restaurant on 125th and Amsterdam was opened and stayed in the same location for thirty-five years.

Food opened the door for deeper cultural and political exchanges.

These Indian restaurants were places where Harlem's Indian community would go to eat, speak Bengali and Punjabi, hang with friends, and discuss the political atmosphere of India and Pakistan. Musicians like Miles Davis frequented the Bombay India Restaurant on 125th to listen to the music being played. In addition, because most Indian restaurants were halal, African American and South Asian Muslims would frequent Indian restaurants for a proper meal.

In the 1950s, Syed Ali, owner of the popular Bombay India Restaurant, married an African-American woman and had two sons of Bengali and African-American descent. They ran the front of

house, and their mother cooked in the back. Not only were the customers in Harlem ethnically and racially diverse, the restaurants were operated by racially and ethnically diverse families. One of the earliest Indian restaurants in Harlem was actually run by two Caribbean men of Indian descent. Because many residents in Harlem had already been introduced to Caribbean and South Asian fare, like curry and roti, it proved to be an easier customer base to develop.

Following the famous Ceylon India Inn's opening on 49th Street in the 1930s, the popularity of Indian restaurants in New York led to an expansion into Midtown's theater district. Other Indian restaurant proprietors followed the same path, and eventually most Indian restaurants moved out of Harlem and into Midtown.

Harlem's diverse culture and population was fertile ground for the Indian restaurant to grow. Not only was it a place to eat, it was a perfect place for cultures to meet. With the linking of cultures, foods, and politics, in both the public and the private spaces, a new Harlem emerged. A roti platter (page 158) is the perfect celebration of Bengali Harlem: a you-can't-get-it-wrong platter of colors and flavors. We encourage you to have your guests eat with their hands.

THE KINGDOM OF

ESSAY
>>>→

Rice stories fascinate us as much as the dishes themselves. Wherever we go in the world, we love to hear how a particular rice dish became a part of the home we're visiting. An example: in Senegal, a woman is making dinner. She is telling a story about the first Indochina Wars. Her grandfather was one of the more than half a million Senegalese soldiers sent to fight, on behalf of France, in 1946. Vietnam was called French Indochina then, and that country, like Senegal, was a colony of France. The woman's grandfather returned home from the war, like many of his contemporaries, with a Vietnamese bride. The woman takes out a picture to show her grandmother: her long and silky jet-black hair, the silk dresses she made at home. The dish she is making is *thiéboudiènne* in French, *ceebu jen* in Wolof, and it means "fish and rice." But it is not just any fish and rice: It is broken rice, fresh fish and dried fish, a fermented spice called *nététou*. You can taste Vietnam in this dish, in the fish and the fermentation, in the broken rice, which is called *com tam* in Vietnam.

If we traveled the world from Africa to Asia and all the points of the diaspora, we could eat only rice and we would not starve. On the contrary, we would feast. We could start on New Year's Day in Charleston, South Carolina, where certainly we would eat hoppin' John, the traditional holiday meal of black-eyed peas and rice, seasoned with a bit of smoked pork. The dish is considered a symbol of good fortune for the year ahead. As culinary historian Jessica B. Harris explains in her wonderful essay "Prosperity Begins with a Pea," although some historians connect hoppin' John to the way it sustained the hungry during the Civil War, "For African Americans, the connection between beans and fortune is surely complex. Perhaps, because dried black-eyed peas can be germinated, having some extra on hand at the New Year guaranteed sustenance provided by a new crop of the fast-growing vines. The black-eyed pea and rice combination also forms a complete protein, offering all of the essential amino acids. During slavery, one ensured of such nourishment was lucky indeed."

South Carolina was called the Rice Kingdom because of the way the colony turned rice into a cash crop in the eighteenth century. Slavery was essential to the production of rice: The work was backbreaking, but even more the slaves were skilled rice farmers who taught the planters how to "properly dyke the marshes, periodically flood the rice fields and use sweetgrass baskets for milling the rice quicker than wooden paddles." But we'd like to reclaim that term, the Rice Kingdom, because rice is so much bigger than its exploitative colonial past.

All around the world, more than 3.5 billion people depend on rice for more than 20 percent of their daily food consumption. Everywhere rice is served, it shows off its diasporic heritage. Sushi in Japan bridges with sushi in Brazil, where Japanese and African immigrants add their flavors to the mix. Paella in Spain shares the same pan-crusty deliciousness as bimbimbap in Korea. Season it with saffron and top the rice with hard-boiled eggs and you've got an Anglo-Indian kedgeree; fry the egg and put it on top of the rice and you've got a Hawaiian loco moco. Cooking the rice in coconut milk is a common thread, from the *arroz con gandules* of Latin America to the *nasi kuning* of Indonesia. Lemon rice in southern India bridges with a lemony risotto in northern Italy. Pilau rice, a play on pilaf, leapfrogs from India to Kenya, where they claim pilau as their own. As we've noted, West Africans are the second largest consumers of rice in the world after Asia: That's one region eating nearly as much rice as a continent that includes China.

What makes rice extraordinary is that we are never simply eating the dish in front of us. Each bowl of rice connects us, grain by grain, to the roads we've traveled and the places we've dined. In Harlem, we are always talking about rice: the best rice we've had recently, new varieties of rice, how to cook all of the many varieties of rice, and what to pair them with. Our Pineapple Black Fried Rice (page 175) is a house favorite that we think you'll soon claim as your own. Our Brown Rice Grits (page 177) is one of those dishes that you can serve for supper, then eat for leftovers at breakfast, and then nibble on the following day as a late-afternoon snack. Our Spiced Goat with Sticky Rice (page 101) is an easy-to-make but impressive dish that works as well with any kind of roasted meat. Our Jollof Rice and Beans (page 178) is a steaming plate of tomatoey goodness that will act as a base for any kind of comfort meal you plan on making.

The poet Nayyirah Waheed wrote, "Can we speak in flowers? It will be easier for me to understand." Rest assured, rice is a universal language. Wherever and however you serve these recipes, you are offering a gift and an invitation: for your guests to share in your rice story and for them to offer up their own.

Coconut Sticky Rice

Sticky rice is a solid base for any savory or even sweet dish, and with this recipe we have both. We've served this many times over the years, sometimes on its own as a side and at others playing a role aside a marquee dish like the whole roasted duck.

Keep the sticky rice covered and warm before serving. It will dry out if left uncovered for too long.

3 cups uncooked sticky rice

2 cups canned unsweetened coconut milk

½ cup sugar

1 tablespoon finely grated lime zest (from about 2 limes)

½ teaspoon kosher salt

6 servings

PREP TIME

2 hours (including soaking time)

COOKING TIME

1 hour 30 minutes

TOTAL TIME

3 hours 30 minutes

Put the rice in a nonreactive container that holds at least twice the volume of the rice: Cover the rice with 2 to 3 inches of warm water and soak for 2 hours.

Drain the rice and place in a steamer basket. Set the steamer basket over several inches of boiling water in a large pot. The rice must not touch the boiling water. Cover and steam for 30 minutes, or until the rice is shiny and tender. Be careful that your pot doesn't run dry during steaming; add more water if necessary.

While the rice steams, pour the coconut milk into a heavy pot and heat over medium heat until it just begins to simmer. Make sure it does not boil. Mix in the sugar, lime zest, and salt, stirring to dissolve the sugar and salt completely into the hot coconut milk.

When the sticky rice is tender, turn it out into a bowl and slowly pour the warm coconut milk over it. Stir gently with a wooden spoon to mix the liquid into the rice, then let stand, covered, for 30 minutes to 1 hour to allow the flavors to blend.

Pineapple Black Fried Rice

This is easily our most popular rice. The pineapple makes it more approachable for newcomers, and just about everyone who's eaten it before asks for it on subsequent visits. It's inspired by the flavored fried rices at Chinese restaurants, but we add our own twists.

Black rice is the key ingredient in this dish, but it can pull some duty on its own, too. As rices go, it does more for the body than just about any other, with high marks for both antioxidants and fiber. Chinese emperors used to corner the market on black rice based on the belief that it helped them live longer. We don't mind sharing.

The secret to great fried rice is using cold day-old cooked rice. After being refrigerated overnight, rice grains will become firm and lose some of their moisture. This makes it easier to separate the grains and less likely that your fried rice will be mushy.

6 servings

PREP TIME
2 hours
10 minutes
COOKING TIME
15 minutes
TOTAL TIME
2 hours
25 minutes

2 tablespoons olive oil
1 large onion, diced (2 cups)
kosher salt
2 cloves garlic, minced
1 bird's-eye chile, seeded and minced
1 cup shelled edamame, cooked
½ cup julienned carrot
1 cup shredded Savoy cabbage

3 cups cooked black rice, refrigerated on a baking sheet for at least 2 hours
1 cup bean sprouts
1 cup small-diced pineapple
2 scallions, sliced
¼ cup soy sauce
1 teaspoon sweet chili sauce

Heat the oil in a large skillet or wok over medium-high heat. Add the onion and season with salt and cook, stirring often, until the onion has become translucent, 2 to 3 minutes. Stir in the garlic and chile and cook until the garlic is fragrant but not browned, about 1 minute.

Add the edamame, carrot, and cabbage and cook, stirring constantly, until the vegetables are tender, 3 to 4 minutes.

Stir in the rice and cook over high heat, stirring to completely incorporate the rice and vegetables. Add the bean sprouts, pineapple, scallions, and soy sauce. Cook over medium-high heat, stirring constantly, until heated through, about 2 minutes. Once all of the ingredients are heated through, press the rice mixture down with your spatula to toast and caramelize the rice. Let the packed rice sit for 2 to 3 minutes, then turn the rice, press, and continue on the other side.

Remove from the heat once the rice is sizzling hot and toss in the sweet chili sauce right before serving.

NOT EVERYBODY CAN COOK RICE *(it takes practice)*

ice is an essential part of the Afro-Asian-American flavor conversation. We take it very seriously. There were certain people at the restaurant who we didn't let cook the rice. Alfredo, for example, was 100 percent not allowed to cook rice. On the other hand, one day, one of our wok cooks called in sick. (Turns out he was driving an Uber on the side.) Melvin, who at the time was our dishwasher, offered to fill in. I said, "No way, Melvin, you can't just jump from dishwasher to wok cook." But it turns out that Melvin, who's from Grenada, has a gift for cooking rice. He grew up cooking with his grandmother. When Tsering, our lead wok cook, who's from Tibet, came back from vacation, he began to train Melvin. Melvin became one of our lead wok cooks. It's in his bones.

Brown Rice Grits

If you're not familiar with grits, you want to make sure to follow the rules: Start with a good amount of water, cook 'em slow, and let them simmer. At the end, you can add a tamarind barbecue sauce (page 87) and you have tamarind barbecue grits. These brown rice grits don't have to be flavored with tamarind; you can cook them with coconut milk or almond butter, or even throw in a handful of your favorite herbs to give the dish a greener, herbier flavor. At home, I like to sometimes skip the tamarind and throw in a spoonful of peanut butter. This is a very versatile recipe.

4 to 6 servings

PREP TIME
5 minutes
COOKING TIME
45 minutes
TOTAL TIME
1 hour

1 cup uncooked brown rice
4 cups oxtail braising liquid (page 84)
kosher salt

Put the rice in a blender or food processor and pulse until the rice is coarsely ground, about ten 5-second pulses.

In a 4-quart saucepan, heat 1 cup water and the braising liquid over medium-high heat and bring to a boil. Slowly add the cracked rice to the boiling liquid, stirring constantly with a wire whisk.

Reduce the heat to low and simmer for 45 minutes, or until soft and creamy. Whisk frequently and taste the grits to ensure they are tender and completely cooked. Season with salt to taste.

Remove from the heat and let the grits rest for 10 minutes before serving.

Jollof Rice and Beans *with* Tomato Sauce

6 servings

PREP TIME
5 minutes

COOKING TIME
45 minutes

TOTAL TIME
50 minutes

Any culture that you want to be a part of has its own version of a one-pot rice dish—jambalaya, paella, and so on—and West Africa's take on the dish belongs with the best of them. From Senegal to Mali, throughout Nigeria, Cameroon, and Ghana, jollof is a beloved favorite. Every cook gives the dish her or his own spin, but what remains consistent is the bright red color that comes from the tomato paste and palm oil. To that base, you can add chicken or fish. Plantains in jollof give it a sweet vegetarian spin. We had it on our menu since we opened in 2013, and it plays the same role as a reliable standard that a hamburger or spaghetti and meatballs would play somewhere else.

2 cups Tomato Sauce
   (recipe below)
1½ cups Adzuki Red Beans (page 188)

2 cups uncooked jasmine rice
1 tablespoon olive oil
½ teaspoon kosher salt

Combine all of the ingredients in a 4-quart saucepan. Add 3 cups water and bring to a simmer over medium heat. Cover the pot and cook for 35 to 45 minutes, until the rice is tender.

Let the rice sit, covered, for 10 minutes after it's done cooking. Then fluff it with a fork.

Makes about 1 quart

TOMATO SAUCE

¼ cup vegetable oil
1 Spanish onion, chopped
kosher salt
2 tablespoons chopped garlic
2 teaspoons chopped fresh ginger
4 bird's-eye chiles, seeded and chopped
½ cup tomato paste
6 ripe plum tomatoes (about 1 pound), chopped

In a 4-quart saucepan, heat the oil over medium heat. Add the onion and sprinkle with salt. Cook until the onion is soft and translucent, 3 to 5 minutes. Add the garlic, ginger, and chiles and cook for 2 additional minutes. Make sure they do not brown.

After the vegetables are softened and begin to release their aroma, stir in the tomato paste and cook for 5 to 8 minutes. Make sure to incorporate the tomato paste with the vegetables to ensure even cooking of the paste.

Transfer to a blender and pulse to combine. Add the chopped tomatoes and puree until the mixture forms a smooth sauce. Add a little bit of water if the sauce is too thick or chunky. Season with salt to taste.

Beer-Battered Long Beans

I t can be hard to fry vegetables as well at home as we do at a restaurant. Start with a nice cast-iron pan. Don't be afraid of turning up the heat. These are in and out of the pan so fast, it's not going to make your house smoky. But you need to get the pan hot enough that the long beans are crispy on the outside and steamed on the inside. Also, you want to serve these immediately.

I like to pair these with our Dibi Short Ribs (page 68), but they can take a starring turn on a vegetable platter with our Purple Yam Puree (page 207) and the Roasted Japanese Eggplant (page 189).

vegetable oil for deep-frying
1 cup rice flour
2 teaspoons kosher salt, plus more for seasoning

1 teaspoon curry powder
1 cup lager beer
1 pound fresh long beans, cut into 8- to 10-inch pieces

In a heavy pot, heat 2 inches of oil to 375°F.

In a large bowl, combine the flour, salt, and curry powder. Whisk in the beer until smooth.

Add a handful of beans to the batter and fold to coat them. Lift the beans out one by one, letting the excess drip off, then carefully add them to the oil. Fry the beans until golden and crispy, 1½ to 2 minutes per batch. Remove from the oil with a slotted spoon and place on a paper towel–lined baking sheet. Season with salt immediately and repeat with the remaining beans.

Okra Fries

6 to 8 servings

PREP TIME
15 minutes

COOKING TIME
10 minutes

TOTAL TIME
25 minutes

Growing up, I hated okra. As I kid, I thought it was slimy and terrible. My first taste of okra fries didn't do much to dispel my childhood aversion. But I kept thinking, "How can I make okra fries good? You never get crispy okra fries." The key here was using cornstarch and rice flour. Cutting the okra in half from top to bottom, the seeds cling to the rice flour and cornstarch so the batter isn't going anywhere. Mariah Carey sampled these okra fries and said they were the best she'd ever had.

The secret to this dish is letting the halved okra pods soak in eggs. Whatever you do, don't skip that part.

vegetable oil for deep-frying
1 pound okra, pods halved lengthwise
1 medium egg, beaten
¾ cup rice flour

¾ cup cornstarch
1 teaspoon smoked paprika
kosher salt

Pour a few inches of vegetable oil into a heavy-bottomed pot, preferably cast iron. Heat the oil to 350°F.

Meanwhile, put the okra in a large bowl and toss with the beaten egg. Let the okra stand for 5 minutes to absorb the egg.

In a separate medium bowl, whisk the rice flour, cornstarch, paprika, and ¼ teaspoon salt. Remove the okra from the large bowl, allowing excess egg to drip back into the bowl, then transfer the okra to the flour mixture. Toss the okra to dredge evenly. Lift from the flour and shake off the excess.

Cook the okra in batches in the hot oil until golden and crunchy, 3 to 5 minutes, depending on size.

Remove with a slotted spoon and place on a paper towel–lined plate. Season with salt immediately. Repeat with the remaining okra.

Charred Okra

O kra is one of those superfoods that we try to use as often as possible. It's an ingredient that tells the story of the African diaspora so well, but one that is also rich in calcium and iron. You want it charred on the outside and tender on the inside. Keep stirring!

6 to 8 servings

PREP TIME
5 minutes
COOKING TIME
15 minutes
TOTAL TIME
20 minutes

2 pounds okra, washed and trimmed but left whole
2 tablespoons olive oil
1 teaspoon kosher salt
½ teaspoon freshly ground black pepper

Use a very large seasoned cast-iron pan or wok and preheat it over medium-high heat.

Make sure the okra is patted dry and toss with the oil, salt, and pepper in a large mixing bowl.

Once the pan is hot enough for a drop of water to sizzle on the surface, add half the dressed okra and cook, stirring often, until charred on the outside and tender when pierced with a fork, 3 to 5 minutes. Transfer to a large plate and repeat with the remaining okra.

Remove from the heat and serve immediately.

Roasted Sweet Potatoes

4 servings

PREP TIME
5 minutes

COOKING TIME
20 minutes

TOTAL TIME
25 minutes

This basic recipe is a great foundation for getting your kids (or your root vegetable–averse significant other) to fall in love with sweet potatoes. Feel free to sprinkle anything you like on top: Brown sugar and crushed pecans are a great way to make this already sweet dish feel like a sweet Southern dessert.

2 sweet potatoes
3 tablespoons olive oil
1 teaspoon kosher salt
½ teaspoon freshly ground black pepper

Preheat the oven to 425°F.

Cut the sweet potatoes in half lengthwise and slice into ½-inch-thick half-moon shapes.

Toss the sweet potatoes in the oil, salt, and pepper and roast on a parchment-lined baking sheet for 10 to 15 minutes.

Once they begin to brown and are able to be pierced easily with a fork, turn the sweet potatoes with a spatula to ensure even cooking on both sides, about 5 more minutes.

After the sweet potatoes are completely tender and lightly crisp on the outside, remove them from the oven and keep warm until ready to use.

Adzuki Red Beans

Makes 3 cups

PREP TIME
15 minutes

COOKING TIME
1 hour
30 minutes

TOTAL TIME
1 hour
45 minutes

This bean dates back thousands of years in Japanese cooking. It's a sweet bean that is used as a filler in many Japanese desserts. Once you start cooking it, you'll find you can use it much the way you might use kidney beans. It mixes well with starches like rice and potatoes, and you can throw it into salads, too.

Don't throw out the cooking liquid after the beans are drained. Save the flavorful and nutrient-rich bean broth to use as a base for sauces or soups.

1 cup dried adzuki red beans
  (red kidney beans are a good
  substitute if you can't find adzuki)
4 cloves garlic, peeled

1 bird's-eye chile
1 Spanish onion, roughly chopped
kosher salt and freshly ground
  black pepper

In a 2-quart saucepan, combine the beans, 4 cups cool water, the garlic, chile, and onion over high heat. Bring to a boil, then quickly lower the heat to a very gentle simmer. You should just see small bubbles through the beans.

Cook over low heat until the beans are tender all the way through, about 1½ hours, adding water as needed to keep beans submerged by at least 1 inch. Make sure to stir the beans occasionally while they simmer, to make sure they don't cook unevenly or burn on the bottom.

Taste the beans frequently, testing their texture and flavor, as they start to become tender after about 1 hour. Season with salt and pepper after the beans begin to soften.

Remove the beans from the heat once they are creamy and soft but before they begin to lose their shape. Cool the beans in their cooking liquid and transfer to a nonreactive storage container. Cover and store in the refrigerator for up to 3 days. Drain the beans from their cooking liquid before using.

Make sure you don't boil the beans or add the salt too early, which will result in uneven cooking.

Lid off vs. lid on: Leave the pot uncovered for firm beans meant for cold salads and pasta dishes. Cover the pot, leaving the lid slightly ajar, for creamier beans for soups and casseroles.

CHEF JJ'S KITCHEN TIPS

Roasted Japanese Eggplant *with* Pecan Bread Crumbs

Regular eggplants can be super bitter, but Japanese eggplants are sweet and worth seeking out. The pecans add a nice nuttiness and take this from a side dish to a main course: a real vegetarian dream.

The key to making simple roasted eggplant extra delicious is to roast it until it's really, really tender and golden. When in doubt, leave it in to roast a little longer.

6 servings

PREP TIME
25 minutes
COOKING TIME
50 minutes
TOTAL TIME
1 hour 15 minutes

4 Japanese eggplants
  (about 4 pounds total)
kosher salt
3 tablespoons olive oil
2 teaspoons ground cumin
1 tablespoon unsalted butter
2 pounds shiitake and oyster
  mushroom mix, minced or
  pulsed in a food processor
1 pint cherry tomatoes, halved
¼ cup Fonio (page 128) or
  cooked millet

1 tablespoon chopped fresh mint
1 tablespoon chopped fresh cilantro
1 teaspoon finely grated lemon zest
  (from about ½ lemon)
Butter Pecan Bread Crumbs (page 191)
  or plain panko bread crumbs
freshly ground black pepper

Preheat the oven to 400°F.

Trim the ends from the eggplants and slice them in half lengthwise. Sprinkle with salt and brush with the oil. Place the eggplants on a parchment-lined baking sheet and roast for 35 minutes, or until soft and completely tender.

While the eggplants roast, heat a large dry sauté pan over medium-high heat. Add the cumin and toast for 3 minutes, or until its aromatics are released. Stir in the butter and add the mushrooms. Sprinkle with salt and cook until the mushrooms soften and release some liquid, about 5 minutes. Stir in the tomatoes and cook for an additional 3 minutes.

Transfer the mixture to a large bowl and gently fold in the fonio, mint, cilantro, and lemon zest and set aside.

Remove the roasted eggplant from the oven and let it cool down enough to handle. Take 2 halves of the eggplant and dice into medium cubes, including the skin. Scoop out the flesh of the other six halves and dice it (reserve the skins). Combine the chopped eggplant with the mushroom and tomato mixture.

Place the 6 scooped-out eggplant shells back on the baking sheet and stuff with the filling. Top with the bread crumbs and return to the oven. Roast for 5 to 8 minutes, until the bread crumbs brown slightly. Grind pepper over eggplant. Serve.

BUTTER PECAN BREAD CRUMBS *Makes ¾ cup*

- 4 tablespoons unsalted butter, cubed
- ½ cup panko bread crumbs
- ¼ cup crushed pecans
- kosher salt

Melt the butter in a 2-quart saucepan over medium heat. Stir in the panko and pecans.

Lower the heat and cook, stirring constantly, until the nuts and bread crumbs begin to turn golden brown and have a nutty fragrance, 3 to 5 minutes. Season with salt and remove from the heat.

Curry Lime Cauliflower

This is one of those sides that make a regular dinner feel special. Curry and lime are a classic combination in Indian cuisine. The cauliflower takes on this beautiful color from the curry, but the lime gives it a tangy sour note that cuts the heat.

1 head cauliflower (2 pounds), cut into bite-size florets
vegetable oil for deep-frying
1 cup rice flour

2 teaspoons kosher salt
1 teaspoon curry powder
1 cup lager beer

4 servings

PREP TIME
10 minutes

COOKING TIME
30 minutes

TOTAL TIME
40 minutes

In a heavy pot, heat 2 inches of oil to 375°F.

In a large bowl, combine the flour, salt, and curry powder. Whisk in the beer until smooth.

Add a handful of cauliflower florets to the batter and fold to coat them. Lift the florets out one by one, letting the excess drip off, then carefully add them to the oil. Fry the florets until golden and crispy, 3 to 6 minutes per batch. Remove from the oil with a slotted spoon and place on a paper towel–lined baking sheet. Season with salt immediately and repeat with the remaining florets.

Serve with Curry Lime Yogurt Dressing (page 50).

Pickled Cabbage Slaw

Makes 5 cups

PREP TIME
15 minutes

PICKLING TIME
1 hour
(or overnight)

You can quick pickle this dish in an hour, but I really recommend making it the night before. Put on your favorite album, take out your cutting board, and three songs in, you'll be done. We serve this in Harlem with our tamarind oxtails (page 87), but it's a great add to your dinner table with almost anything. It's the perfect cooling touch for the days when it's too hot to cook. But it's also great to whip out in the winter when the offerings of fresh produce can be unreliable.

½ cup white wine vinegar
¼ cup soy sauce
¼ cup sugar
¼ cup kosher salt
1 bird's-eye chile, seeded and minced
1 carrot, julienned

1 daikon radish, julienned
2 cucumbers, cut in half and sliced into thin half moons
½ head Savoy cabbage, thinly sliced
3 tablespoons minced fresh cilantro

Whisk together the vinegar, soy sauce, and 1½ cups water with the sugar, salt, and chile in a large bowl. Whisk until the salt and sugar are completely dissolved and set aside.

In a nonreactive container, toss together the carrot, radish, cucumbers, cabbage, and cilantro. Pour the brine over the vegetables and cover. Refrigerate for 1 hour or up to 1 week. The slaw will become more pickled as it rests.

Spicy Black-Eyed Peas

This dish infuses traditional black-eyed peas with the Afro-Asian flavors that are at the heart of this book: cumin and cilantro, bird's-eye chile and lime. You can use canned peas for ease and not sacrifice any of the bold flavors. It's a comforting weeknight dish that will also hold pride of place at any Sunday supper.

2 tablespoons olive oil
½ cup diced red onion
kosher salt
5 cloves garlic, minced
½ cup diced carrot
½ cup diced celery
1 bird's-eye chile, diced, with seeds
1 teaspoon ground cumin
¼ cup canned chipotles in adobo, with their sauce

2 tablespoons chopped fresh cilantro
3 cups cooked black-eyed peas, or 2 (15-ounce) cans black-eyed peas, rinsed and drained
4 cups vegetable stock
juice and zest of 1 lime, zest removed in large pieces with a vegetable peeler (1½ tablespoons juice)
freshly ground black pepper

In a 6-quart pot heat the oil over medium-high heat. Add the onion, sprinkle with salt, and cook for 3 to 5 minutes. Stir in the garlic and sauté for 2 minutes. Add the carrot, celery, chile, and cumin and cook for 2 additional minutes.

Add the chipotles in adobo and break the chiles up with a wooden spoon. Bring to a simmer and and cook to reduce the sauce down for 1 minute.

Add the cilantro and peas, then pour in the stock. Add the lime juice and zest and bring to a simmer, then lower the heat to medium.

Let the beans simmer for about 30 minutes, uncovered, until the sauce is reduced but the beans still hold their shape. Remove the pieces of lime zest. Season with salt and pepper to taste and serve.

Makes 6 cups

PREP TIME
20 minutes
COOKING TIME
40 minutes
TOTAL TIME
1 hour

Yam Flapjacks

Growing up, I was not a flapjack fan: too dry, too crumbly, too flavorless. Our recipe is the ultimate flapjack rethink. Yam, a West African staple, not only thickens the batter but adds a creaminess that traditional flapjacks lack. Vanilla extract adds that taste of Madagascar. Exotic yet homey and familiar at the same time.

1¼ cups all-purpose flour
2 teaspoons baking powder
¼ teaspoon kosher salt
1 cup buttermilk
¼ cup packed dark brown sugar

2 large eggs, lightly beaten
1 tablespoon olive oil
1 teaspoon vanilla extract
¾ cup roasted and mashed yams
vegetable oil for cooking

6 to 8 servings

PREP TIME
20 minutes

COOKING TIME
10 minutes

TOTAL TIME
30 minutes

Combine the flour, baking powder, and salt in a large bowl. Whisk in the buttermilk, brown sugar, eggs, olive oil, and vanilla extract. Stir until just incorporated and add the mashed yams to form a thick batter. Set the batter aside to rest for about 10 minutes.

Heat a large nonstick pan or griddle over medium-low heat. When the pan is hot, grease with about 1 teaspoon vegetable oil. Cook the batter in batches of silver-dollar pancakes (about 2 tablespoons of batter per pancake). Cook until the edges of the pancake look shiny and dry and the bubbles that form in the batter begin to pop, 2 to 3 minutes. Flip the pancakes and continue cooking until puffed in the center and golden brown, about 2 minutes. Keep the flapjacks warm while you cook the remainder.

Roasted Cipollini Onions *in* Coconut Yassa

Yassa poulet is one of the national dishes of Senegal. What I did was use the yassa as a marinade instead of as a base for a stew. So you get all that flavor in whatever protein or vegetable you put in this marinade. There's lemon, mint, mustard, bird's-eye chile, and, while it's not traditional to the yassa, a little bit of soy sauce to amp up that umami flavor.

We take our yassa marinade and add coconut milk to give you more of that traditional Senegalese yassa flavor. We love it with roasted cipollini onions, but you can pour it on top of your favorite meat. It's just one of those versatile sauces you can use for everything.

6 to 8 servings

PREP TIME
5 minutes
COOKING TIME
45 minutes
TOTAL TIME
50 minutes

2 tablespoons olive oil
2 pounds cipollini onions, peeled and
  sliced
kosher salt and freshly ground black
  pepper

1 cup Yassa Marinade (page 200)
1 cup canned unsweetened
  coconut milk
1 tablespoon fresh lime juice

Preheat the oven to 325°F.

Heat the oil in a large cast-iron skillet over medium heat. Add the onions and stir to coat. Season to taste with salt and pepper. Transfer to the oven and roast, stirring occasionally, until deeply caramelized and tender, about 30 minutes.

Carefully remove from the oven and place on the stove over medium heat. (Make sure to cover the hot handle with an oven mitt.) Stir in the marinade and coconut milk and bring to a simmer. Simmer the sauce and onions until reduced by half and the sauce thickens, about 15 minutes, stirring occasionally. Add the lime juice and season to taste.

Makes 2 cups

PREP TIME
10 minutes
TOTAL TIME
10 minutes

YASSA MARINADE

¼ cup loosely packed fresh mint leaves

¼ cup soy sauce

½ onion, chopped (1 cup)

1 teaspoon finely grated lemon zest (from about 1 lemon)

1 bird's-eye chile, seeded and chopped

1 teaspoon fresh thyme

1 teaspoon Dijon mustard

¼ teaspoon kosher salt

¾ cup vegetable oil

Put all the ingredients in a blender and pulse to combine. Make sure to keep the marinade chunky and add a touch of water if it is too thick.

Store the marinade in an airtight nonreactive container in the refrigerator for up to 4 days.

25

Pickled Red Onions

This quick pickling recipe will work on almost any vegetable you choose and will keep in the fridge for five days, making it a go-to for sandwiches and salads all week long.

⅓ cup champagne vinegar
2 tablespoons sugar
1½ teaspoons kosher salt

1½ teaspoons coriander seeds
1 large red onion, thinly sliced
   into half moons

Combine the vinegar, 1 cup water, the sugar, salt, and coriander in a 2-quart saucepan over medium-high heat, whisking until the sugar is completely dissolved, and bring to a rolling boil. Lower the heat and allow the pickling liquid to simmer gently for 5 to 8 minutes.

In a nonreactive, heatproof pint-size container, carefully pour the boiling hot liquid over the onion, covering it completely. Let sit until cooled to room temperature.

Once the onions have cooled to room temperature, cover with an airtight lid and store in the refrigerator until needed.

Makes 2 cups

PREP TIME
5 minutes
COOKING TIME
8 minutes
TOTAL TIME
13 minutes

House-Made Pickles

Makes 3 pints

PREP TIME
1 hour

PICKLING TIME
3 days minimum

Daikon radish. Collard greens. Okra. Cucumbers. Baby carrots. When we whip up our house-made pickles, it's like we're all transported to Alexander's grandfather's farm in Spartanburg, South Carolina. Pickling is having a moment, and it's easy to see why. An hour's worth of chopping and boiling means your family gets to enjoy something homemade and delicious for weeks to come.

½ cup cider vinegar

½ cup champagne vinegar

4 cloves garlic, peeled

2 bay leaves

2 bird's-eye chiles

¼ cup sugar

1 tablespoon kosher salt

1 tablespoon coarsely ground coriander seeds

1½ to 2 pounds of any of the following:

• Cucumbers, sliced or speared

• Okra, whole, with the stems trimmed

• Collard greens, stems only, cut into 2-inch pieces

• Daikon radish, peeled, halved, and sliced into half moons

• Baby carrots, stems trimmed, halved lengthwise

In a 2-quart saucepan over medium heat, combine the vinegars, 2 cups water, the garlic, bay leaves, chiles, sugar, salt, and coriander. Bring the mixture to a boil, stirring to dissolve the sugar and salt. Once boiling, pour the mixture over the vegetables in sterilized glass canning jars and seal so the jar is airtight.

Store in the refrigerator for at least 3 days before serving. Keep refrigerated.

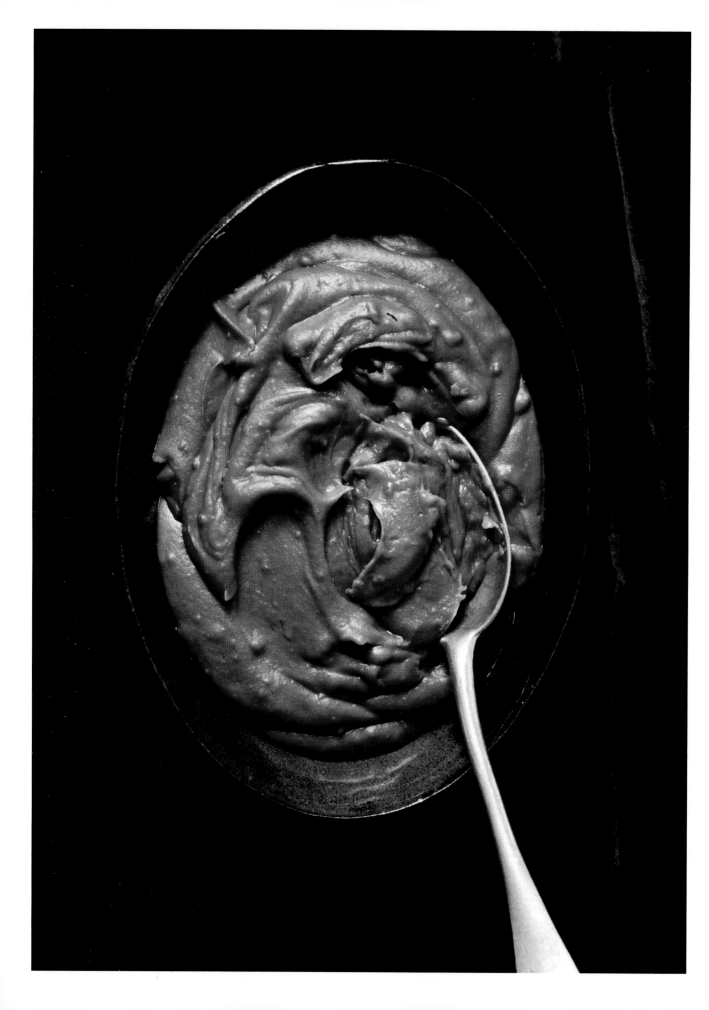

Purple Yam Puree

Yams grow in so many different colors. You'll see orange, purple, and white—especially in the fall. This dish is creamy, sweet, and colorful. The coconut milk and butter add layers of flavor. Then we mix in cinnamon and cayenne pepper to kick up the spice a little bit. When you top it with the crushed walnuts, it's the very epitome of a restaurant-quality dish that you can easily make at home.

6 servings

PREP TIME
10 minutes
COOKING TIME
35 minutes
TOTAL TIME
45 minutes

2 to 3 large purple yams (about 2 pounds), peeled and chopped
⅓ cup canned unsweetened coconut milk, warmed, or more if needed
4 tablespoons unsalted butter, melted
kosher salt

2 tablespoons maple syrup
¼ teaspoon ground cinnamon
pinch of ground cayenne
freshly ground black pepper
Spiced Walnuts (page 34), crushed (optional)

Put the yams in a 6-quart pot and cover with cool water. Bring to a boil over medium-high heat. Boil until fork tender, 20 to 25 minutes.

Drain the yams and return them to the pot. Add the coconut milk, melted butter, and ¼ teaspoon salt and mash with a potato masher or with a hand mixer until smooth and creamy, adding a touch more coconut milk if needed. Stir in the maple syrup, cinnamon, and cayenne. Season to taste with salt and pepper. Scoop the mashed yams into a large bowl. Top with the spiced walnuts, if using, and serve.

Apple Cider-Glazed Brussels Sprouts

e gave our apple cider glaze an African touch with palm sugar, cinnamon, and bird's-eye chile. This is one of those aromatic dishes that will make your kitchen smell like heaven.

1 pound Brussels sprouts
¼ cup extra-virgin olive oil
5 cloves garlic, peeled

kosher salt
½ cup Apple Cider Glaze (recipe below)
freshly ground black pepper

6 servings

PREP TIME
10 minutes

COOKING TIME
35 minutes

TOTAL TIME
45 minutes

Preheat the oven to 400°F.

Trim the bottoms of the Brussels sprouts to remove the tough stalk, and slice each in half top to bottom.

Heat the oil in a cast-iron pan over medium-high heat until it shimmers; put the sprouts in the pan cut side down and don't stir. Add the garlic and sprinkle with salt.

Cook, undisturbed, until the sprouts begin to sizzle and brown on the bottom, about 5 minutes, then transfer to the oven. Roast, stirring occasionally with a spatula, until the sprouts are quite brown and tender, 15 to 20 minutes. Stir in the glaze and cook for 5 more minutes to caramelize the glaze.

Taste, and season with salt and pepper. Serve hot or warm.

Makes ½ cup

PREP TIME
10 minutes

COOKING TIME
35 minutes

TOTAL TIME
45 minutes

APPLE CIDER GLAZE

1 cup apple cider
1 tablespoon palm sugar (or dark brown sugar)
1 teaspoon minced fresh ginger
½ bird's-eye chile, seeded and minced
½ cinnamon stick
1 tablespoon apple cider vinegar

Combine all the ingredients in a 2-quart saucepan over medium heat. Whisk to dissolve the sugar and bring to a simmer.

Simmer, without boiling, until the glaze is reduced by half and thickened, about 20 minutes. Strain through a fine-mesh sieve before cooling; discard the solids.

Store in a covered nonreactive container in the refrigerator for up to 5 days.

Poached Pears *in an* African Nectar Tea Broth

The secret to this dish is red rooibos tea. In West Africa, it's considered a cure-all for everything from insomnia and headaches to asthma and hypertension. As a chef, I love the aesthetic quality of the rich red broth and its deep nutty flavor.

4 African Nectar rooibos tea bags (red herbal tea)

1 stalk lemongrass, bruised and chopped

1 Spanish onion, chopped

½ teaspoon chopped garlic

1 tablespoon chopped fresh ginger

zest of 2 lemons, removed with a vegetable peeler

zest of 2 oranges, removed with a vegetable peeler

1 Asian pear, diced with the peel on

1 bird's-eye chile, coarsely chopped

3 tablespoons soy sauce

1 cup sugar

3 cinnamon sticks

¼ cup champagne vinegar

3 tablespoons kosher salt

2 teaspoons freshly ground black pepper

4 firm Bosc pears, peels left on, halved, core scooped out with a spoon

4 to 8 servings

PREP TIME
20 minutes

COOKING TIME
1 hour
15 minutes

TOTAL TIME
2 hours
(including
cooling time)

In a 6-quart pot, combine all of the ingredients except the pears with 2 quarts water and bring to a rolling boil. Lower the heat to medium and let simmer for 45 minutes to 1 hour to bring out the aromatic and slightly spicy, tangy, and sweet flavors.

Pour 2 cups of the liquid and solid ingredients (avoiding the cinnamon sticks), into a blender and carefully blend until smooth. Stir the warm puree back into the liquid in the pot.

Place a strainer over a separate large pot and carefully pour the liquid through the strainer; discard the solids.

Bring the liquid back to a simmer and add the pear halves. Cover and simmer for 12 to 15 minutes, until the pears are just tender when poked with a skewer or the tip of a knife.

Remove the pears and reserve the liquid. Let cool and store separately in the refrigerator in covered large plastic storage containers for up to 4 days if you're not serving immediately.

Or chill and serve in Daikon Radish Salad (page 32).

Asian Pear *and* Plum Kimchi

Fermented vegetables are this beautiful bridge between West Africa and Asia. You'll see a fermented sweet potato in West Africa that is so much in line with the pickled plums (umeboshi) of Japan or the pickled mangos (achar) that they make in India. Canning and pickling vegetables is a way of preserving the harvest all around the world. This dish plays on the traditions of Korean kimchi: building on the base of pickled cabbage and daikon radish and throwing in some black-eyed peas, Asian pear, and some beautiful red plums. You can play around with the mix of fruit and legumes.

6 servings

PREP TIME
25 minutes
PICKLING TIME
2 to 3 days

1 head Savoy cabbage, shredded
1 daikon radish, grated
1 cup bean sprouts
1 cup cooked black-eyed peas, or canned black-eyed peas, rinsed and drained
1 cup black currants
4 red plums, quartered and sliced
4 Asian pears, quartered and sliced

¼ cup julienned fresh ginger
½ bunch fresh cilantro, stems removed
2 tablespoons kosher salt
¼ cup sugar
1 cup soy sauce
1½ teaspoons spicy chile paste
¾ cup rice wine vinegar
1 cup sweet sake wine
3 tablespoons fish sauce

Gently toss together the vegetables, peas, fruits, ginger, and cilantro in a large nonreactive container.

In a separate bowl, whisk together the remaining ingredients, making sure everything is dissolved and well combined.

Pour the marinade over the vegetable mixture and cover. Let stand at room temperature for 2 to 3 days before using to get the full potency of the marinade.

RED HOT SAUCE, YELLOW HOT SAUCE

by JJ JOHNSON

In the summertime, we'd go visit my grandfather's sister in Queens. That was the Barbados side of the family. Every summer, they'd have a big barbecue pig roast: the whole hog. That was the highlight of my summer.

The women would be filling up jars with dried fruit and putting Bajan rum in with the fruit. Then at Christmastime, they would use that fruit to make rum cake. The adults would give the kids rum cake if they were acting too crazy to try to calm them down and make them go to sleep, because literally you could get drunk off of that cake.

I remember the two sides of my family from the kinds of homemade hot sauce they made. The Puerto Rican side made a red, vinegary hot sauce with pickled and fermented peppers. The Barbados side made a yellow hot sauce that was super spicy.

My grandmother passed away when I was still very young, but I think her soul lives in me, with respect to the food. I live my life doing the things she loved to do: cook, feed people, eat good food, and drink wine. I like to think that my grandmother would be proud of me. But I am also fairly sure that she looks down on me from heaven and she says, "If you'd had more time in my kitchen, you would be an even better chef than you are now. And for sure, your Spanish would be better."

SAUCES, DRESSINGS & JAMS | 215

Collard Green Salsa Verde

To keep the vibrant color of the salsa verde, hold off on adding the vinegar until just before serving to avoid oxidation and discoloration.

kosher salt
1 bunch collard greens,
    coarsely chopped
¼ cup Brazil nuts
1 head garlic, cloves peeled

1 tablespoon finely grated lemon zest
    (from about 1 lemon)
½ bunch fresh parsley,
    coarsely chopped
1 cup olive oil
½ teaspoon rice wine vinegar

Bring a 10-quart pot of water to a rolling boil and add ½ teaspoon of salt. Fill a medium bowl with equal parts ice and cold water.

Quickly blanch the collard greens in the boiling water for 1 minute. Drain in a colander in the sink and quickly plunge the greens into the ice bath to immediately stop the cooking and maintain a bright green color. Remove the greens from the ice bath and squeeze out any excess water.

In a food processor, finely grind the Brazil nuts until they make a smooth paste that resembles the consistency of creamy peanut butter, about 1 minute. Remove the paste and set aside.

Wipe out the food processor and add the garlic, lemon zest, and parsley. Pulse until the garlic is finely minced. You can use a flexible rubber spatula to scrape down the ingredients in the food processor to make sure everything mixes evenly.

After the garlic mixture is thoroughly combined, add the collard greens and pulse five times for a chunky and not pureed mix.

Once incorporated, slowly add the oil while pulsing the food processor in short bursts to combine without overblending. Add the Brazil nut paste and pulse two or three times to just combine.

Add salt to taste (I use about 1½ teaspoons) and stir in the vinegar just before serving.

4 to 6 servings

PREP TIME
10 minutes
COOKING TIME
5 minutes
TOTAL TIME
15 minutes

Bourbon Apricot Dried Fruit Compote

Makes 3 cups

PREP TIME
20 minutes

COOKING TIME
30 minutes

TOTAL TIME
1 hour

Alexander loves bourbon. We were hanging out at his house, envisioning the menu for the restaurant. He served me bourbon, and there were dried apricots on the table. I realized how well those two ingredients would go together.

This will keep in the fridge for up to ten days. Once I whip up a batch, I tear through it pretty quickly. I'll use it in the morning on my toast. Then at dinnertime, I'll reach for it again as a glaze for steak. Forgot to make a dessert? Spoon this compote on top of a bowl of vanilla ice cream. Even though it has peppers and onions, with ice cream it'll give you this beautiful salty-sweet moment.

This is a dish you can't really get wrong. Just chop everything, throw it in the pot, let it simmer, and stir, stir, stir.

1 cup chopped dried apricots

¼ cup pitted dates, quartered

¼ cup dried currants

¼ cup golden raisins

½ red onion, julienned

¼ cup bourbon

1 Asian pear, peeled and cut into ½-inch cubes

1½ cups chicken or vegetable stock

juice and zest of 1 lemon, zest removed with a vegetable peeler

½ teaspoon kosher salt

Combine all the ingredients in a 4-quart saucepan over medium heat. Cover partially and simmer, stirring frequently, for about 30 minutes, until the fruit is nicely plump and reconstituted. Let cool completely before using, then transfer to a container, cover, and refrigerate.

Bird's-Eye Chile Jam

This is all about using old techniques to cook up new flavors. This is a spicy, syrupy West African jam that will work well as a dipping sauce for bread as a starter or a snack. We serve it with chicken liver pâté (page 102) in Harlem, but you could use it as an accompaniment for any kind of grilled meat or grilled plaintains.

10 bird's-eye chiles,
  seeded and chopped
2 tablespoons olive oil
2 cups granulated sugar
2 tablespoons palm sugar
  (or dark brown sugar or cane sugar)

2 tablespoons finely grated lemon zest
  (from about 2 lemons)
1 teaspoon kosher salt
3 tablespoons apple pectin
1 bunch scallions, thinly sliced

Puree the chiles and oil in a blender until smooth. Set aside.

In a 2-quart saucepan, combine the sugars over medium-low heat. Heat the mixture, without stirring, until the sugar melts down to a syrup-like consistency.

Carefully add the lemon zest, chile mixture, and salt.

Slowly pour in 2 cups water while stirring and cook over medium heat to bring to a boil.

When the mixture begins to boil, quickly whisk in the pectin. Continue whisking until the pectin is completely dissolved.

Boil the jam for about 10 minutes, stirring occasionally with a wooden spoon, and remove from the heat to cool. The liquid will appear syrupy while it's hot but will gel as it cools.

Allow the jam to cool down completely before adding in the scallions so that they keep their bright green color. Store in a jar in the refrigerator.

If you're unsure when the jam is ready to cool, remove the pan from the heat and place a spoonful of the jam on a chilled saucer and put it in the fridge. Wait a few minutes and check to see whether it's begun to firm up. If it's still runny, continue to cook the jam.

Makes 2 cups

PREP TIME
5 minutes
COOKING TIME
35 minutes
TOTAL TIME
40 minutes

CHEF JJ'S
KITCHEN
TIPS

Piri Piri Sauce

This sauce only requires 30 minutes of your time, but you want to give it your full attention. For the flavors to blend and emulsify, you need to add each ingredient slowly and give it a full 10 minutes of whisking toward the end. It'll keep in your fridge for five days, and you'll use it on everything.

¾ cup extra-virgin olive oil

1 yellow onion, diced

3 cloves garlic, minced

1 tablespoon minced fresh ginger

4 bird's-eye chiles, minced and seeded

1 habanero pepper, minced and seeded

3 plum tomatoes, diced (1½ cups)

2 tablespoons tomato paste

juice and finely grated zest of 2 oranges (¾ cup juice, 1 tablespoon zest)

kosher salt and freshly ground black pepper

Makes 2 cups

PREP TIME
10 minutes

COOKING TIME
20 minutes

TOTAL TIME
30 minutes

In a large sauté pan, heat 2 tablespoons of the oil over medium-low heat. When the oil is hot, add the onion, garlic, ginger, and bird's-eye and habanero chiles and slowly cook, stirring occasionally, for 8 to 10 minutes, until the vegetables are soft and the onion is translucent. Add the diced tomatoes and tomato paste and continue to cook until tomatoes are soft, about 5 minutes.

Stir in the orange juice and zest. Lower the heat and simmer the sauce until thickened, 10 to 15 minutes. Remove from the heat.

Drizzle in the remaining oil while whisking constantly to form a creamy sauce. Set aside to cool, then store in an airtight nonreactive container in the refrigerator for up to 5 days.

Kaffir Daiquiri

This is a classic with an African twist. Strong, sweet, sour. Aromatic and balanced. Easy to drink.

6 servings

TOTAL TIME
10 minutes

1½ cups white rum
½ cup fresh lime juice
½ cup simple syrup (½ cup
  boiling water poured over
  ½ cup sugar to dissolve),
  cooled

5 kaffir lime leaves
  (or peeled zest from 1 lime
  and ½ stalk lemongrass,
  bruised)
GARNISH: kaffir lime leaves

Prechill six martini glasses.

Combine all the ingredients in a 1-quart mason jar with a lid. Shake vigorously with ice and strain into the chilled martini glasses. Garnish with lime leaves.

Blood *and* Fire

6 servings

TOTAL TIME
5 minutes

This tequila cocktail mixes cucumber and hibiscus: a combination that's complex with a sharp, tangy edge.

1½ cups white tequila
½ cup Hibiscus Syrup (page 135)

½ cup fresh lemon juice
GARNISH: long cucumber slices

Combine all the ingredients in a 1-quart mason jar with a lid. Shake vigorously with ice and strain into rocks glasses over ice. Garnish with cucumber.

Jasmine Blossom

This botanical gin cocktail gets its great floral aroma from the combo of white peach puree and lime juice. Careful with this one: It goes down easy.

6 servings

TOTAL TIME
5 minutes

1½ cups gin, floral and dry
½ cup white peach puree

⅓ cup fresh lime juice
⅓ cup agave syrup

Combine all the ingredients in a 1-quart mason jar with a lid. Shake vigorously with ice and strain into rocks glasses over ice.

Oleo Saccharum Demerara

This syrup is the base for any citrusy cocktail you might want to make. We like to serve them in an old-fashioned punch bowl; it will be almost like your bar is transported into a 1920s speakeasy. But make sure to warn your guests: The lemony sweetness does a brilliant job of masking the alcohol content in the drink.

zest of 4 lemons, removed with a vegetable peeler
1 cup sugar

Remove any white pith from the strips of lemon zest.

In a medium bowl, gently crush the zest with the sugar using a wooden spoon or muddler until combined. Let the mixture rest overnight, covered, at room temperature.

Strain the liquid into an airtight container, pressing on the peels to extract as much liquid as possible. Cover and refrigerate for up to 1 month.

West African Peanut Punch

6 servings

TOTAL TIME
10 minutes

Y ou've never had anything like this rich bourbon cocktail. The peanut base makes it creamy, spicy, and salty.

¾ cup roasted peanuts

1½ cups bourbon

¼ cup chile honey (store bought, or you can make your own by warming 1 cup honey with 1 tablespoon chile powder for 5 minutes and then letting it cool)

GARNISH: roasted peanuts

Put the peanuts and 2 cups water in a blender. Blend on high until the mixture is completely smooth.

Strain into a large chilled pitcher. Stir in the bourbon and honey, making sure the honey is completely dissolved.

Serve over ice and garnish with peanuts.

Sweet Tea Julep

6 servings

TOTAL TIME
5 minutes
(not including
lemon oil)

This is our riff on the mint julep. Subtle tea notes and lemon throw a curveball on the classic.

½ cup lemon oil (Oleo Saccharum Demerara; page 227)
1½ cups black tea–infused rum

½ cup fresh mint leaves
GARNISH: mint sprigs

Fill six chilled mint julep cups with crushed ice.

Combine all the ingredients in a 1-quart mason jar with a lid. Shake vigorously with ice and strain into the prepared julep cups. Garnish with mint sprigs.

Black Tea–infused Rum

1½ cups white rum

2 black tea bags or 2 teaspoons loose black tea

Steep for 15 minutes; strain and store in an airtight nonreactive container until ready to use

Minton's then: **Thelonius Monk is to the far left, in his trademark beret.**

Minton's
PLAYHOUSE

Richard "Dick" Parsons always loved jazz. He was especially smitten with the supper clubs of the 1950s and '60s, when good music and a good plate of food were both just an arm's length away. He says, "I took my senior prom date to a place called the Hickory House, and we heard Billy Taylor. And I still remember it. It was my first adventure in being a grownup, to listen to some good jazz." By the 2000s, jazz hadn't left Harlem, but the supper clubs were in decline. There were some jazz venues, but "most of them you wouldn't go to eat. And the elegance has kind of left the building."

St. Nick's Pub, which opened in the 1960s, closed in 2011. The popular Lenox Lounge, which was once home to such luminaries as Billie Holiday, Miles Davis, and John Coltrane, shut down in 2012. When we decided to reopen Minton's Playhouse, it was a tremendous opportunity to bring together the most important elements of the African-American experience: the jazz, the food, our social sensibilities, our creativity, our liveliness, all on this fantastic corner on 118th Street and St. Nick's.

The Cecil Hotel was a hot spot of Harlem in the Roaring Twenties. But what made it transform from infamous to legendary was Minton's Playhouse, the jazz and supper club that opened on the first floor of the hotel in 1938. Henry Minton was a tenor saxophonist who knew that in the early days of jazz, musicians needed a place where they could play the music they liked, push the limits of the genre, and get a good plate of food at the end of the night. He opened Minton's with the specific intent to feed the jazz musician: literally and figuratively.

The circumstances of Henry Minton's life made him a good godfather to jazz. He was the first African-American musician to be invited to serve as a delegate to New York's powerful musician's union, the American Federation of Musicians, Local 802. He had also served as manager for the Rhythm Club, frequented by musicians like Louis Armstrong and Fats Waller. It was that mix of business acumen and union credibility that helped Minton's Playhouse thrive in the golden era of jazz. The musicians' union was fond of handing out exorbitant fines to musicians who dared to play outside of their purview. Dizzy Gillespie remembered that the punishment for playing in a jam session could be a fine of anywhere between a hundred to five hundred dollars: a huge amount of money for the time. Yet jam sessions were at the very heart of the evolution of jazz; improvisation and the spontaneous gathering of a diverse mix of talented instrumentalists were essential to the development of what would become the jazz canon. At Minton's, because of Henry's union associations, musicians could jam without fear of union repercussions.

This freedom to create attracted the best and the brightest. The house band at Minton's was led by Thelonius Monk and Kenny Clarke. The two men set the bar so high that the *New York Times* noted, "Their bucking-bronco tactics threw some of the musicians right off the stage. The ones who stayed included Dizzy Gillespie, Coleman Hawkins, Don Byas, a Juilliard student named Miles Davis, and Charlie Parker, who had a notable ability to put away fried chicken."

Teddy Hill, the manager at Minton's, was a former bandleader with deep connections to two Harlem institutions, the Savoy Ballroom and the Apollo Theater. Hill began to invite performers over to Minton's on Mondays, their usual night off. Dizzy Gillespie recalled, "On Monday nights, we used to have a ball. Everybody from the Apollo, on Monday nights, was a guest at Minton's, the whole band. We had a big jam session. Monday night was the big night, the musician's night off. There was always some food there for you. Oh, that part was beautiful. Teddy Hill treated the guys well."

Welcome to Harlem:
A Jumping Cultural Conversation with Alexander, JJ, and Veronica

VERONICA: I can't even remember the first time I met Alexander. He's been in my life since the days of Cafe Beulah, and I knew about him through mutual friends like the artist Lorna Simpson and Studio Museum director Thelma Golden.

But I distinctly remember the first day I went to Minton's to meet JJ. I was wearing a red shirt, denim shorts, and some red heels. I thought, not a big deal.

Then I got up to Harlem, I was waiting outside because I was a little early. This car full of guys rolls by, and they call out, "Oh, you're so dressed up!" I thought *Okay. Didn't think so, but okay.*

Then a woman walked by and she said, "I like the way you matched your top with your shoes."

Then a few minutes later, an older woman walked by and she said, "Now, ain't your hair pretty?"

I was so struck that in the course of five minutes, I'd interacted with all of these total strangers and they'd been so warm and complimenting. It was so unexpected.

ALEXANDER: **Welcome to Harlem.**

VERONICA: Yes. Welcome to Harlem!

JJ: *That's what I was about to say, "Welcome to Harlem."*

VERONICA: I had worn that outfit a thousand times that summer downtown, and nobody said nothing. But the love in Harlem was immediate and real. When I've been away from Harlem for a little while, I forget about the warmth, about the way people interact, the way that they break down boundaries that exist in other places.

ALEXANDER: Let me say this, as a precursor. Harlem made such an impression on my father before he married my mother, that when I was a kid growing up, he would tell Harlem stories to me every Sunday morning on the side porch.

VERONICA: Wow.

ALEXANDER: **Harlem was the magic city, and I came to New York with these preconceived ideas about a dressed-up place, uptown somewhere in Manhattan, where black folks shine. It was like being in the South, but you're in the North with sophistication.**

VERONICA: It's like that saying from the 1920s, I'd rather be a lamppost in Harlem than the governor of Georgia.

ALEXANDER: **In Harlem, everybody dressed. It was almost like a private circle of people who dressed for each other and inspired each other. So, coming to Harlem, and giving presence to what you just said, folks in Harlem understand style; they appreciate when people go beyond just the usual, and those elements are part of the language and communication. You'll start a conversation with somebody just because you admire their**

shoes. I mean, nothing breaks the ice better, because there's this incredible appreciation for people who put on the dog, go a little extra.

JJ: *There is this presence of being in Harlem. You're supposed to be the finest all the time. You never are supposed to let your guard down. You make sure you have creases in your pants. That is what I used to get screamed at about. I still get screamed at about that from Alexander–not having creases in my pants.*

ALEXANDER: Dressing well is really Harlem. On Sundays, I remember I used to love to go to the House of Prayer because I'd want to be sitting right there when the church was let out, and there'd be the parade of festive colors, and textures, and hats, and gloves, and spit-shined shoes, and two- and three-button vests. Laid out to perfection. This is the community of Harlem.

VERONICA: JJ, could you talk a little bit about the area, because you were living in Harlem before you started working at The Cecil and Minton's, right?

JJ: *My aunts lived in Harlem, my grand-mother lives in Harlem, everybody lived in Harlem. Not knowing I would ever cook in Harlem. Harlem is always a jumping, cultural conversation place. If you say hello to somebody, people say hello back. It was one of the few places in New York City that reminded me of home like the Poconos. You walk into a store, and everybody says hello to you.*

ALEXANDER: That is how Harlem is. Some-body always said hello to you, always said good morning. Nobody just walked by you or bumped you on the street like every-body knows New York to be.

JJ: *When I would walk to work from where I live, that same old lady would say hello to me in the morning or wave to me from the window on my way to work. Sometimes, somebody stops me in the street or a doorman flags me down to say, "I read about you in the newspaper. Keep up the good work." There is always that sense of support and community. That is why I feel it is the greatest community in the world.*

VERONICA: Alexander, when you were thinking about this venture with Mr. Parsons, did you know that people would want to stop by on their way home from work, want to have their first dates here, want to meet up on Sunday? Did you know how the restaurant would live in the community?

ALEXANDER: In a way I did, because Harlem is just a mirror reflection of a Southern town.

VERONICA: Can you say more about that? Preferably while somebody brings me more of your famous mac and cheese?

ALEXANDER: All of those practices and rituals and sort of customs and traditions observed in Harlem came from mostly the Carolinas. It came from the southern migration. Harlem was always just a bigger Southern town in the North.

This was the first time for me to open a restaurant north of 42nd Street . . . I had never had a restaurant in Harlem, and I knew it would be different because I also knew how African Americans responded to my other restaurants that were

downtown. For example, I knew on Sunday I was going to get a larger grouping of African Americans who saw my restaurant on 19th and Park as a destination, because when black folks are dressed, they are ready to go somewhere.

VERONICA: That's the double truth, Ruth.

ALEXANDER: You know, church gets you ready but then you got the rest of the day. It's only one o'clock. We got to go somewhere, and we did the same thing in the South. Part of it was the Sunday parade of people who would just kind of walk around so they could show off their outfits.

VERONICA: Right. JJ, could you talk a little bit about what Sunday in the restaurant was like?

JJ: *Like Alexander said, people are coming from church, and they are really showing off. It just happens that we'd have jazz playing in Minton's, so it really keeps that church spirit going. It's packed, and everybody from Grandma and Grandpa to the little kids are really dressed up while they are eating.*

VERONICA: You talked about the intergenerational diners. Are there dishes that kids love as much as the grandparents do? Are there some dishes you just think are universal in families?

JJ: *I think a universal dish is the cinnamon-scented guinea hen (page 59). They will tell their kids, "Oh, it's just like fried chicken."*

VERONICA: Right.

JJ: *They do love cinnamon, so they kind of trick them and then later on say, "You know you ate guinea hen when you were eight years old?" Or you get those sophisticated eaters like your daughter who comes in, Veronica. Kids like your daughter just want to try something new or they love wild striped bass or they like a bowl of spicy black beans. They know how to relate to the dishes. They might not know the history, but they understand some of the flavors.*

ALEXANDER: On Sundays, Dandy Wellington comes in dressed to the nine, him and his band every Sunday. Three vests, two coats, a hat, a sweater.

VERONICA: Wow. His name is Dandy Wellington?

ALEXANDER: Yes, he is quite an icon on the New York scene.

VERONICA: Nice. So let's talk about music. What to you is the soundtrack of Harlem?

JJ: *Alexander is way better than me about music. I think of Afro beats, I think of '90s hip-hop. Lauryn Hill is always playing in the streets of Harlem somewhere.*

VERONICA: That's great. How about for you, Alexander, what are the songs and artists that seem to you iconic to Harlem and to the restaurant?

ALEXANDER: Iconic to Harlem, anything Nina Simone. Sort of Nina Simone meets Miles Davis. Those sounds, that style, is what the Harlem music scene is based on. Dizzy Gillespie, Monk, you know, that kind of encompasses not only the period music but also that music that was the foundation for bebop, which is what Minton's is all about. The great Motown sound, Otis Redding and Sam Cooke. All of those things to me kind of set the table for Harlem music, both Renaissance and what has been sort of graduating to what is contemporary.

(ALEXANDER CONTINUES) When I think of Afro-Asian-American cooking, I think of a more global expression of music. Like JJ said, Afro-pop but also Felt and Afro-Cuban and Brazilian music, a lot of the music of Bahia, the pressing of drums, the sounds of Jamaica, all of those Caribbean drums, steel drums.

VERONICA: I love that. I want to ask you guys, if you were hosting your ideal dinner party, uptown, in Harlem? Let's say the two of you can invite anyone to dinner, who would you invite and what would you serve?

ALEXANDER: I would have the same guests. You go first, JJ, because you know we wouldn't have the same guests.

VERONICA: Oh, yes, okay. Let's start with JJ.

JJ: *If I could invite anybody, I would invite my grandmother, who is no longer here, because I think she would adore and love this experience that Alexander created with my help here. Barack Obama and Michelle, of course, because we haven't had them yet. I would say world leaders that really respect culture, and I am trying to think of one. I would definitely say Stevie Wonder.*

VERONICA: That sounds like a dinner I'd like to go to.

ALEXANDER: So, let me tell you about my dinner party.

VERONICA: Yes, please.

ALEXANDER: Are you ready?

VERONICA: I'm ready.

ALEXANDER: You know, because I gave it some thought.

JJ: *I can only imagine who you are going to say now.*

ALEXANDER: I know, right? Well, you said one of my people already. But, I would have a dinner party with Toni Morrison, James Baldwin, Barack Obama, Nina Simone, Langston Hughes, Leontyne Price . . . and Abe Lincoln.

VERONICA: Wow!

JJ: *Abe Lincoln?*

ALEXANDER: Abe Lincoln.

VERONICA: Bring it on, Abe!

ALEXANDER: Bring it on! The Gettysburg Address got him invited.

VERONICA: I love that. What would you serve?

JJ: *What wouldn't we serve, right Alexander?*

ALEXANDER: Right. Most notable: she-crab soup with sweet corn fritters.

VERONICA: Yum.

ALEXANDER: Shrimp gumbo and banana pudding pie.

JJ: *I'll make all the drinks.*

ALEXANDER: [laughs] You get to make mint juleps.

VERONICA: Okay, I love that, and I want to be on that guest list.

ALEXANDER: Alrighty.

VERONICA: I wanted to ask, what is your favorite time of day in Harlem and what is your favorite table in the restaurant?

JJ: *I can answer Alexander's favorite table. My favorite time of day in Harlem is the morning, because you really see the culture of the people that live in Harlem.*

VERONICA: By morning, you mean what time?

JJ: *Between like eight and ten. The streets are full, the kids are going to school, the parents are dropping them off, people are getting on the train, people are getting ready to go downtown, and it is really full of life and culture. My favorite table in the restaurant, I would say, underneath the Geisha . . . What is that, forty-two–no, fifty-two?*

ALEXANDER: No, that is fifty-nine.

JJ: *So then I can see everyone with my back to the window. Fifty-nine, yes.*

VERONICA: That is your favorite table?

JJ: *Yes, because I can sit there and literally see it all. The whole restaurant. How people eat, who's walking in, who's walking out, who looks happy, who looks sad, and I can really see it all sitting there.*

VERONICA: But you don't sit down. I notice that when I come in the restaurant.

JJ: *No, that is just respect to everyone that is working. When I am working, I don't sit down. When I come in with friends or family or just to check out the food and the service, that's where I like to sit.*

VERONICA: Okay. Alexander, what is your favorite table in the restaurant, and what is your favorite time of day in Harlem?

ALEXANDER: I created seventeen as my favorite table, and it became everybody else's.

VERONICA: Everybody wants to be where you are, Alexander.

ALEXANDER: Including Dick Parsons. Table seventeen.

VERONICA: Why is it your favorite?

ALEXANDER: It is kind of in an alcove. I like spaces where there is nothing on one side of me. It is like a little nook. It's really like an L-shaped kind of seating.

VERONICA: Right, I love it. What is your favorite time of day in Harlem?

ALEXANDER: My favorite time of day in Harlem is between five and seven a.m.

VERONICA: Why is that?

ALEXANDER: The city is just starting to wake up. I love that. I love feeling like I am part of something new that is about to happen. I like to get out before when JJ was saying when the city is alive and people are going to school and going to work. I am done by then.

JJ: *You are done by then! Well, you wake up at like four thirty in the morning. People are getting in from the club and you are waking up.*

ALEXANDER: The point is, by seven, seven thirty a.m., the city is no longer mine. In that little moment, that time of day, it is all mine. I love that. I really do.

Appendix

RESOURCES

BLACK GARLIC: Garlic that is fermented in its skin, black garlic takes on a deep caramel flavor; buy it in vacuum-sealed bags at Japanese markets, some Trader Joe's locations, or online.

FONIO: An ancient, tiny grain of West Africa, a cousin of millet; fonio has the potential to become a staple grain. Find it in specialty stores and online.

GREEN PEPPERCORNS: Pickled green peppercorns can occasionally be found in the pickle section of the grocery store and should not be confused with capers, which look similar. Order them online.

HARISSA: A chile and spice paste or dried spice blend that usually includes ground red chiles (mild or hot), cumin, caraway, cinnamon, black pepper, and garlic; available at some grocery stores in the spice or condiment aisle or online.

HIBISCUS FLOWERS: The red petals of the flowers in dried form; they can be found pulverized in tea bags or whole.

STICKY RICE: Not to be confused with other short-grain rice varieties, sticky rice, aka glutinous rice or sweet rice, is grown in Southeast Asia. The grains look opaque or matte. Find it at Asian, especially Thai, grocery stores or online.

TAMARIND: The sticky contents of seeded tamarind pods, tamarind paste tastes like sour molasses, and lime juice is a common, though less interesting, substitution.

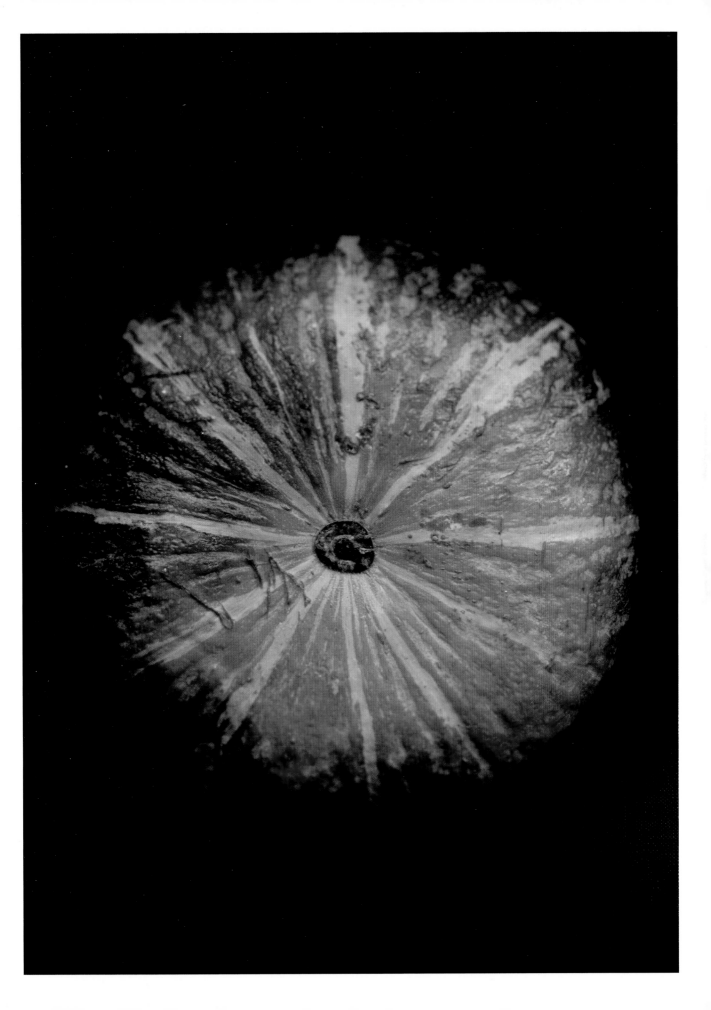

Alexander's Acknowledgments

This book speaks to the contributions of extraordinary people . . . families and communities of doers and achievers. Those who gave of themselves beyond what they imagined was possible, not knowing their lives would create a lasting legacy. Our goal here, and always, is to celebrate the foodways of the African diaspora. By tracing the steps of our ancestral people, we fuse together a culinary conversation in the kitchen. We pay homage to the crossroads of their lives through food and culture, bringing attention and reverence to their influence on global cuisine. Hopefully, and humbly, paying tribute to years of unsung people who gave so much of themselves and received so little in return, who went unnoticed and unappreciated, enslaved for centuries throughout the world.

As we thank them, acknowledge them, and remember them, we want to thank as well the many partners, collaborators, supporters, and special people who helped us realize and create every aspect of this journey . . . the recipes . . . the restaurant, and this manuscript we serve . . . this cookbook.

I'd like to start by thanking all those people who told me I could never be what I have become because they never understood what it was I was becoming—thank you!

My parents and my host of relatives: uncles and aunts, grandparents who cooked and farmed, sharing the lessons of their trials and struggles. You gave me the hope and determination I built my life upon. Your willingness to allow me to be the odd child that I was—curious, insatiable, trying, exhausting—was nothing short of a gift. Thank you. You were determined, even unwavering, in your dedication to allowing me to be my own unique creation, for that I thank you.

I want to sincerely thank Laura and Richard Parsons, my friends for over twenty years now, for their friendship. Their great generosity, enthusiasm, and financial support allowed me to develop, create, and foster the wealth and breadth of this Afro-American-Asian food journey. A special thanks to Laura Parsons, whose guiding hand and encouragement was the silent hand moving this project forward.

You made sure this opportunity happened for me. Love you, Laura, so much! Laura and Richard, I'm thankful for your willingness to engage and for giving me permission to tell this culinary story. The journey we are on has meant the world to me. I will be forever grateful to you both.

I want to thank Joseph "JJ" Johnson, originally my chef de cuisine, then the executive chef of The Cecil and Minton's, for joining me in the pursuit of flavor and historic heritage. Thank you for partnering with me, believing in an old guy with a dream. You brought a passionate commitment to the task at hand, and in the process, we created unsung culinary treasures. We traveled to the Motherland, brought back the Mother Africa Sauce, and opened a restaurant kitchen of the finest quality. I appreciate you, all you gave and sacrificed to help me realize the power of an idea. I will always be grateful.

To my great friend Paul Goodman, who has more than supported me and my many projects, his counsel has been essential. When the Parsons and I decided to open The Cecil and Minton's, Paul was one of the first people I called. Having had him as my legal champion when I opened my third restaurant in Grand Central Station, I knew I needed him on my team and he delivered.

In the midst of all the hard work it took to make this dream come true, I took a holiday trip to the Dominican Republic. There, I met the owner of the beautiful resort Casa Colonial, Sarah Garcia. Sarah, who has become one of my most cherished friends, is a brilliant architect, designer, hotelier, and extraordinary personality. She was the mastermind designer who gave life to these two spaces. Her interpretation of decor and design with a mixture of heritage and modern touches was exactly what I was looking for. After convincing the Parsons that she was the one . . . she became the one. She was joined by the New York and Atlanta–based architect Tonja Adair. Tonja was our boots-on-the-ground tactician, a problem solver and architect of record. Tonja, we thank you for both the vision and the hard work.

Thank you to Beatrice Stein, a restaurant pro and longtime friend. Beatrice has been a part of all five restaurants I have owned. She has been with me from the beginning, and when it was time to put together a team to get the job done, there was no other consideration for me. Her loyalty and work ethic are what make her indispensable. I could have never opened two restaurants a month apart if she was not the one behind the scenes pulling the strings. An enormous debt of gratitude for her hard work and dedication. Thank you, Bea, for being you for all seasons.

Thanks to John Simoudis, art designer and brand developer, who tirelessly gave us the best of himself.

A special thanks to Tiffany Minter, our beloved sous chef, then chef de cuisine, whose audition for the job at the restaurant was in my kitchen in Harlem. I bought a restaurant stove to create and test all the recipes. Tiffany, a very shy and composed chef, blew us away with her preparations and dedication. She has been an incredible part of the foundation of who we are, and I am truly appreciative for her work and commitment to our story.

I'm thankful for Veronica Chambers for her ability to capture the spirit of our story while leaving the voice intact. You supported the narrative with intellect, insight, and care, and added greatly to the telling of this story. Veronica, you're an important ingredient in this recipe.

Special thanks to my literary agent and friend for more years than not, Victoria Sanders. Her dedication, support, and guidance has helped create an outlet for my artistic and literary expression, and her devotion to my career has made me better. Thanks to her great team of professionals who get what the job really is . . . and get it done.

A big thanks to Will Schwalbe of Flatiron Books and his amazing team of enablers and enhancers: Kara Rota and Bryn Clark. Your vision and passion for this project is what brought us here. Looking forward to book number two!

With appreciation to Beatriz da Costa, who captured the photogenic vision of our mission. You brought to life every dish on a page. Roscoe Betsil, your stylistic approach to food on a plate made all the difference every shot—a big thank you! Roberto de Vicq, your beautiful design is incomparable. And thanks to Dana Walcott and Mary-Frances Heck. Your expertise ensures that everyone will make the same dish every time.

There are so many others! Too many for us to measure, who joined us, supported us, and gave so much to the cause from the very beginning. Friends and loved ones. Our first group of staff members and managers, both in front and back of house. A handful of professional practitioners, consultants, people who were simply there when we needed them. A special thank you to Jim Deal (Executive Director of H.S.I.) and landlord, the Cecil Tenants who were our first customers. Curtis Archer, President of HCDC; Terry Higgins, builder; Larry Vanore, man of numbers; and Rosa Brito, whom I am so very proud of for having worked her way up from office worker to senior management team. And lastly, the Harlem Community where I live and belong . . . Thank you, Harlem, for your support and fulfilling my dream. You make it real: this space we inhabit between uptown and heaven.

JJ's Acknowledgments

I want to thank Mr. and Mrs. Parsons. They believed in me through Alexander. You came and tasted the food I cooked, then let me run not one, but two restaurants. Thank you for believing in me.

This all started in Alexander's apartment: an extraordinary place that is all at once a culinary think tank, an artists' salon, and a historical archive dedicated to the African diaspora. Alexander opened a door for me that no one else would. He gave me a kitchen when it was very hard to become a chef in New York City. But more than that, he gave me the best gift of all. He let me cook the food of who I am. Alexander, thank you for this. My first hire was Alfredo, one of the first guys I trained as a young cook in New York City. Then it was Jessica, my lead line cook, who worked with me at my previous post. I wanted this to be a diverse kitchen (still a rarity in big New York restaurants) made up of people who would balance each other out. Tim Cooper joined us and created this amazing bar program. He also introduced me to Tiffany Minter. Tiffany, I don't have to say it in a book for you to know that you are our backbone. You understood from day one and were the perfect partner in this project. Thank you, Josh Ozersky: you put me on the map.

The Cecil, where this journey began, was more than a restaurant, it was a home. Every employee who has worked at Cecil, I thank you. This book could not have been written without you. Juan, you are the real MVP. You took all the yelling and the screaming, and you pushed to be one of the best sous chefs working today. I see me in you. Thank you.

The dishwashers! We could not do it without you. Beatrice Stein, we've got so much love for you. Lisa Cash, you jumpstarted us. Thank you for running up and down the stairs every time I needed a manager. Rosa, you have become a Swiss Army knife. The tears we have shared! Luz, Amarando, Roman, Andres, Mamaoud, Melvin, Tsring, Reina, Wendy, you made it happen every day, and I thank you. Love to everyone that has been through this journey, thank you!!!! As ever, push, push, push!!!

I want to thank my wife, Mia Chapman, who showed extraordinary grace and unending support during this process of long nights and early mornings. She tasted recipes and new creations of mine. She is my favorite person to cook for. I love you, Mia.

My parents and my wonderful extended family always believed in me. From culinary school to the frantic opening of two restaurants, their support has been unwavering.

It was amazing to work with Veronica Chambers. She has made me look at food in ways that I never had before. Veronica pulled the emotion I have for these dishes out of me and helped me bring them to the page.

Will Schwalbe, Beatriz da Costa, Roscoe Betsil, and Roberto de Vicq are great minds who helped the book come together in a visual and creative way. And we couldn't have done this without the passion and support of Kara Rota and Bryn Clark.

Index

header